VIRGINIA
DISTILLED

VIRGINIA
DISTILLED

———— ✦ ————

Four Centuries of Drinking in the Old Dominion

PATRICK EVANS-HYLTON

AMERICAN PALATE

Published by American Palate
A Division of The History Press
Charleston, SC
www.historypress.com

First published 2021

Manufactured in the United States

ISBN 9781467144285

Library of Congress Control Number: 2021943424

Notice: The information in this book is true and complete to the best of our knowledge. It is offered without guarantee on the part of the author or The History Press. The author and The History Press disclaim all liability in connection with the use of this book.

CONTENTS

ACKNOWLEDGEMENTS

I was born during the *Mad Men* era of imbibes (also called the "Dark Ages of Cocktails") in the middle part of the twentieth century, when two-martini lunches rolled effortlessly into happy hour after work. The weekend dance card was filled with boozy brunches and crazy cocktail parties.

My earliest memories of dining out with my folks, in fact, involved cocktails. When we'd go out to one of the ubiquitous, mid-priced steakhouses for that special occasion, my father would always order a whiskey sour. Before the fizz deflated on top, he'd push the glass my way and let me slurp off the foam and snack on the brilliantly hued maraschino cherry garnish. And when his sister would come visit and the family all made our way out to brunch, I would chomp on the vodka-soaked celery stick from her bloody mary.

I myself had my own ritual. I recall with clarity sitting down at Steak Manor, looking over the clown-shaped children's menu (maybe that's one reason I detest clowns to this day) and glancing up at our waiter. "Tommy," I'd say with authority and familiarity, "I'll have the hamburger steak, and let me start with a Shirley Temple." While the adults in the dining room all enjoyed their drinks, us kids did too. But I did not know then what I know now—that a cocktail is much more than a liquid way to relax. Along with its intoxicating components, it has a deep-rooted history, especially in Virginia. That is what we explore in this book.

I have been writing about eats and drinks professionally since 1995, and along the way, there have been many friends who have been my champions. I am forever indebted to my late husband, Wayne Hylton, with whom I shared more than a quarter century (and many cocktails) until his passing in 2016. He was with me at the beginning of my writing career and was my tireless champion and muse. His support and words continue to resonate through me with each project I am engaged in.

Many thanks to bartender extraordinaire Karl Dornemann for crafting the prepared cocktail photos in this book, as well as for providing the location for the photo shoot at Still Worldly Eclectic Eats in Portsmouth, one of the restaurants he and his partner, Eric Stevens, own and operate. Much gratitude, too, to Lucas Pomianek for excellent photos of the prepared cocktails and to Stella Pomianek of Café Stella in Norfolk for providing the food shown in the images.

Thank you as well to my companion, Douglas Stisher, for his love and support in my career and throughout the writing of this book. Doug has also been instrumental with project research.

And to my four-legged love, my Chihuahua, Miss Pico De Gallo, thank you for all the kisses and snuggles as you sat next to me while I worked.

Also, a big thank-you to my acquisitions editor at The History Press, Kate Jenkins, for her friendship, guidance and support though this process. Those also assisting throughout the process include the amazing Amy Ciarametaro, executive director of the Virginia Distillers Association; bon vivant Jim Roberts; and the wonderful bartenders and distillers across the Commonwealth.

INTRODUCTION

More than thirteen thousand years ago, our ancestors came upon an amazing find: sometimes fruit, as it decayed, would take on a magical quality. The liquid produced in the process of it breaking down had a slight bite to it, and there was a warm feeling when it was consumed. After a while, a sense of euphoria took over. The liquid was wine.

For a good part of our human experience, beer, mead and wine were consumed for a number of reasons. Sometimes it was just for sheer enjoyment. Sometimes it was taken for medicinal use and other times as part of a ritual. Other times still it was seen as safer to drink than water and consumed as such.

These early drinks didn't require a lot of fuss or human involvement, but as techniques advanced, they became more refined and regarded.

Distilled spirits were a completely different animal. They required advanced materials and technology, and they most likely weren't developed until sometime well after beer and wine were being drunk. By the fifteenth century, alchemists, monks and physicians were routinely practicing the craft, and although they were largely used for medicinal purposes, a growing number of folks drank for enjoyment.

By the time Captain Christopher Newport arrived in 1607 with his crew of 103 boys and men at Cape Henry in present-day Virginia Beach as a stop before firmly establishing the Virginia colony, distilled spirits were being widely enjoyed. The English had always been a drinking lot, be it beer, spirits or wine. But early in the days of the colony, when it was little more than the fledgling, fortressed Jamestown and some outlying plantations, being self-sufficient with spirits and wine was elusive, and much of what Virginians drank was imported—and expensive.

Beer was crafted, as it was seen as not only necessary for pleasure but also as a safe alternative to perceived contaminated drinking water. But *vinifera* grapes did not grow here, and the wine was described as having the taste of wet dog. Things changed in 1620, when colonist George Thorpe distilled the first batch of whiskey made from corn—what he called "corn beere"—at present-day Berkeley Plantation, making it the first liquor crafted in what would become English-speaking America. This was the ancestor of both moonshine and bourbon.

Over the next four centuries, Virginia's relationship with distilled spirits grew. It reacted to events within the state and across the nation: expansion, revolution, civil war and the war on drinking known as Prohibition.

Today, the Commonwealth is firmly established as the "Birthplace of American Spirits." World-class bartenders shake and stir creative cocktails crafted from a wide range of offerings from the eighty-some distilleries that dot the landscape from the Chesapeake Bay to the Blue Ridge.

Cheers to Virginia.

Chapter 1

THE SEVENTEENTH CENTURY

VIRGINIA: THE OLD DOMINION

Be merry my hearts, and call for your quarts,
and let no liquor be lacking,
We have gold in store, we purpose to roare,
untill we set care a packing

London was a crowded, dirty city of about 200,000 folks at the turn of the seventeenth century. Packed, noisy streets were shared with man, woman and child as well as dogs, cats, rats and other animals, making their way to and fro, eking out a living. Accidents, "consumption" (tuberculosis), "French pox" (syphilis), "jaw fain" (tetanus) and the plague were out to get you in a time when the average life expectancy was just thirty-five years old.

No wonder the English loved their drink, gathering in countless inns and taverns across the city, raising tankards and bellowing out drinking songs from thin, poorly printed sheets costing a penny each with lyrics such as those above, from "A Health to All Good-Fellowes," carried to the tune of "To Drive the Cold Winter Away."

But gathering together for a drink wasn't just a time to forget your sorrows—it was a time to celebrate, a time to gather with friends and a time to dream—much like today. This was a time of dreaming, with talk of a voyage to the New World in the air.

"Colonists Leaving England for Jamestown," as shown in this vintage postcard. *Author's collection.*

The English had been there before, establishing the short-lived Roanoke Colony in what is now Dare County, North Carolina, in 1585. But a perfect storm of being ill-prepared and establishing poor relations with the Native Americans seemed to doom the settlement from the start. When a detachment that had sailed to England for supplies returned in 1587, barely a sign of what is commonly known as the Lost Colony remained.

Despite the failed attempts in the past, in 1606 King James granted a proprietary charter to the Virginia Company of London for the establishment of colonies in the New World. The company hired Captain Christopher Newport to take command. The call went out along the wharfs and through the taverns for an ample number of boys and men to fill the three ships that would set sail that year. Perhaps it was with a glass of genever or other aqua vitae that those voyagers found the courage to sign on to such an adventure.

Five days before Christmas 1606, Newport gathered on the cold, windy docks in Blackwall, an area in east London. Joining him were 144 boys and men in the ships *Susan Constant*, *Godspeed* and *Discovery*. The ships pushed away, sailing down the Thames River, into the English Channel and out into open sea. It was a long journey of four months on the small vessels, which made their way past the Canary Islands just off the coast of Africa before turning westward toward the West Indies. Each sailor was given food rations and a gallon of beer per day.

A long history between the Caribbean and Virginia, including a lasting influence on food (including distilled spirits) and foodways, began as the ships made their way through the Caribbean. They called port at Martinique, Dominica, Guadalupe, St. Croix and Puerto Rico among them, picking up supplies. They turned north, well off the coast of Florida, and spotted the capes that form the entrance to the Chesapeake Bay.

The English had been here before, as well as the Dutch, exploring the coastline of America. In 1570, Spanish Jesuits even established the short-lived Ajacan Mission, believed to have been near present-day Yorktown.

On April 26, 1607, Newport guided the ships off Cape Henry, currently in the present-day city of Virginia Beach. They anchored, and the crew made their way ashore. On the sandy beach, among the wind-blown dunes, with the air kissed heavy with salt from the surf, the captain planted a cross in honor of England in an event called the "First Landing." Thus Day 1 on what would become the first permanent English-speaking settlement on North America had begun.

The next day, the colonists explored, and George Percy (1580–1627), the crew's diarist and future governor, wrote about encountering Native Americans roasting oysters who fled when they saw the Englishmen. There they "left many of the Oysters in the fire. We ate some of the Oysters, which were very large and delicate in taste." More exploration brought other finds, including a "ground full of fine and beautifull Strawberries, four times bigger and better than ours in England."

But this area of Virginia left the colony open to attack from the sea, especially by the Spanish. In a few days, Newport gathered the boys and men and sailed farther inland, passing between the present-day cities of Newport News and Norfolk and turning northward up what would later be known as the James River. After a short time, they found an area that seemed to meet their needs geographically and explored the region around it for a week. Then, on May 14, the colonists took root at Jamestown Island.

The settlers right away took to building a fort for protection around their collection of buildings, although many were not use to hard, physical labor, which made the task that much more formidable. Also against them was the fact that although the peninsula of land on which they were establishing the colony provided a strategic location in the river, and although the river channel around it was deep enough for navigation, there were other issues. The water was brackish and stale, making it non-potable and also a haven for disease-carrying mosquitos. The land wasn't much better—it was considered poor for agriculture by Native Americans. Regardless, the colonists had arrived too late in the season to plant crops for this first year, and many also lacked farming skills (and, for that matter, fishing and hunting skills).

The pressure was on from another viewpoint: the Virginia colony was meant to be a moneymaking enterprise; the colonists hoped to have time to search for and manufacture valuable goods to ship back to England. Trade with the Native Americans for food was established but often problematic. The settlers also anticipated regular supply ships coming from England, but it took considerable time for those to arrive. On top of it all, droughts and other natural disasters conspired against them, and by 1609–10, in the "Starving Time," some 80 percent of the folks at Jamestown had died.

Relief came for the colony in 1612, when it was discovered that tobacco not only grew in the sandy, loamy soil in Virginia but actually thrived. Tobacco became an important cash crop because of high demand in England.

The colony expanded, and by 1624, the charter of the Virginia Company had been revoked. King James transferred the royal authority to form a crown colony. At this time, a muster roll showed a total population of 1,281, with 124 of those living in Jamestown itself. Of the total population, about three-fourths of those were male.

Virginia outgrew the small area in and around Jamestown, and other settlements opened up—some to the south such as in the present-day cities of Norfolk and Virginia Beach, some to the west such as in current Isle of Wight and Surry Counties and others north along the James River, snaking their way toward where Richmond is today. Jamestown would be abandoned in favor of Williamsburg and, later, Richmond.

Exploration of western lands, and grants for land in those regions, moved others out of Virginia's low country into the rolling Piedmont, across the Blue Ridge Mountains into the Shenandoah Valley, across the Allegheny Mountains and onward. At one point, across the Virginia territory, a number of partial or whole other states were included: Illinois, Indiana, Kentucky, Minnesota, Ohio, West Virginia and Wisconsin. Virginia itself achieved statehood on June 25, 1788.

Today, the Commonwealth, affectionately known as the "Old Dominion"—a nickname given by King Charles II—stretches for almost forty-three thousand square miles from the Atlantic Ocean and Chesapeake Bay across open fields and thick forests to the rolling, rounded tops of the ancient Blue Ridge Mountains and deep along the floor of the Shenandoah Valley. Some 8 million folks call themselves Virginians, and at last count, some six dozen distilleries or more carry on the rich tastes and traditions of craft spirits established in this special land at the very beginning of our nation.

Raise a Glass: Beer

Virginia was, first and foremost, a British colony, and that was at the heart of what was on the plate and in the glass for a good time after the First Landing.

Because the colony was so remote from Mother England, improvisation also played a part in Virginia eats and drinks. The merging of traditional English foods and foodways with Native American established a fusion that became the first true American regional cuisine in what would become English-speaking America. In short order, the same influence would be felt with Virginia's strong Caribbean connections.

From Native Americans, however, there was no influence with alcohol; most indigenous peoples of North America neither produced nor used alcohol, and for those who did, they were mostly limited to the present-day southwestern United States and Mexico. But the impact on spirits in the New World from the Caribbean about a half century after the First Landing cannot be understated, as the colonies developed a taste for rum.

Seventeenth-century England—and, by default, Virginia—loved to drink. People drank beer, wine and distilled spirits. "Colonial Americans, at least many of them, believed alcohol could cure the sick, strengthen the weak, enliven the aged, and generally make the world a better place. They tippled, toasted, sipped, slurped, quaffed, and guzzled from dawn to dark," said Ed Crews in "Drinking in Colonial America" for the *Colonial Williamsburg Journal*. He added, "Many started the day with a pick-me-up and ended it with a put-me-down. Between those liquid milestones, they also might enjoy a midmorning whistle wetter, a luncheon libation, an afternoon accompaniment, and a supper snort. If circumstances allowed, they could ease the day with several rounds at a tavern."

Beer was a common beverage in eighteenth-century Virginia. It was the everyday drink for most people, principally for enjoyment but also for health reasons. Water was often contaminated, and a weak beer, safe for drinking since the water was boiled in the process, was crafted for everyday consumption. Beer came with the first settlers, who celebrated deciding on the Jamestown spot for their fort with beer, wrote diarist George Percy.

"Alcoholic drink was one of the few items that colonists could not live without. In a place where the water was unsafe, milk was generally unavailable, tea and coffee were too expensive for all but the very wealthy, and soda and nonalcoholic fruit juice were not yet invented, alcoholic beverages were all that colonists could drink safely," noted Sarah H. Meacham in her book *Every Home a Distillery: Alcohol, Gender, and Technology in the Colonial Chesapeake*.

In fact, when they did drink the water, George Percy noted in 1609, "Our drinke [was] Cold water taken out of the River, which was at a floud verie salt, at low tide full of slime and filth, which was the destruction of many of our men." But the solemnness of the situation was not lost on Captain John Smith, who wrote in his *Generall Historie of Virginia* that "[b]eing thus left to our fortunes…there remained neither tavern [nor] beer-house."

Regretfully, the London Company failed to send a brewer along with the others, just one of the problems faced. There was frustration as they waited for additional beer to come from England. Sir Francis Wyatt, the first governor, placed an ad in a London newspaper calling for two brewers to come set up their craft. Crops of barley were planted in anticipation of their arrival. Many of the brews crafted were a kind of near beer, a weak beer consumed, along with cider, as part of everyday living. But there was always an appetite for a strong ale too.

By 1609, spotty records indicate that a small pub or tavern was operating in the colony. In his 1729 diary, *History of the Dividing Line*, Virginia author, planter and statesman William Byrd II mused, "Like true Englishmen, they built a church that cost no more than 50 pounds, and a tavern that cost 500." In the 1649 *A Perfect Description of Virginia*, of which the author is unknown but may be John Farrer, the writer noted, "That they have Six publike Brewhouses, and most brew their owne Beere, strong and good."

Frank Clark, historic foodways supervisor for Colonial Williamsburg, noted that records later in the colony's history from the Governor's Place in Williamsburg indicate that beer was brewed on site and that imported beers were stored there as well. He added that home brew was rationed to servants and slaves, while the imports were kept for the governor and guests.

It wasn't unusual for most folks to brew their own; there was a limited number of commercial brewers in Virginia at the time, and many households created their own beer with ingredients we'd recognize today: grain, water, hops and yeast. But Clark said that malted barley wasn't easy to come by in Colonial Virginia, so brewers improvised with what they had at hand like pumpkin, molasses and sometimes even spruce and pine. Beer, wine and other drinks were largely improvised with what ingredients were available, as noted in these lines from a seventeenth-century poem:

If barley be wanting to make into malt,
We must be content and think it no fault.
For we can make liquor to sweeten our lips,
Of pumpkins, and parsnips, and walnut-tree chips.

Beers then would have been more bitter than today's brew because of the increased amount of hops present—both as a flavoring and a preservative. Also, Clark noted that because of ingredient quality inconsistencies, as well as lacking a standard recipe, the brew would have most likely tasted different from batch to batch as colonialists drank it from leather, pewter or earthenware mugs or tankards.

Raise a Glass: Wine

Colonists first tried to make wine in 1609 with gathered, uncultivated grapes, producing nearly twenty gallons. They took a drink and promptly regretted it. The would-be imbibers described the taste as foxy and the fragrance as that of a wet dog and proclaimed the first vintage undrinkable. The grapes were probably native scuppernong and not a variety of *Vitis vinifera*, which produces the quality wines associated with European vintages.

They tried, and tried again, but by 1618, the settlers had abandoned the idea of making wine with native grapes altogether, and the Virginia Company brought more than eight French vines and winemakers, or *vignerons*. Those efforts failed too—a combination of the European vines not being suited to the hotter, more humid climate in Virginia as well as introduction to a new host of disease and pests that killed them off.

High-priced imported wine like claret, sack, sherry, Canary, Malaga and Tent from France and Italy were enjoyed by the upper class, but most colonists drank ale and beer because they were unable to afford the imports.

After a while, the momentum for producing commercial wine was lost, but it was not abandoned. In 1769, the General Assembly in Williamsburg, at that point the capital of Virginia, passed "An Act for the Encouragement of the Making of Wine." Encouragement notwithstanding, the effort failed due to pests and disease. The onset of the American Revolutionary War also played a part.

About this time, the state also purchased one hundred acres of land in York County to establish a winery. It brought over French winemaker Andrew Estave and promised him the deed to the property if he could produce ten hogsheads—630 gallons—of quality wine within six years. He was unable to do so. But a good deal of information was harvested nevertheless—Estave found that it was the vines themselves that were the problem, noting that while the French vines withered in summer heat and were destroyed by a host of insects, black rot and mildew, native grapes seemed to do just fine.

The conclusion: if a suitable microclimate could be found—one that closely matched the vine's native French countryside—and if productive pest-control methods were established, then it was time for making wine. Among those who sought answers was Thomas Jefferson, whom many consider to be America's first wine connoisseur. Jefferson, the third president of the United States, was a true oenophile with a dream of turning Virginia into a major wine producing state.

Intoxicated with all things French, Jefferson served in that country as ambassador and spent much of this time learning the skills of winemaking. He wanted to successfully grow the *Vitis vinifera* in Virginia and produce quality, European-style wines in America.

Enter Italian viticulturist Filippo Mazzei. Jefferson brought him to Monticello in 1773 to plant and nurture vines from France. They cleared a tract of land—the current site of Jefferson Vineyards—but Mazzei could not nurture the plants past disease and climate conditions. Jefferson did not live to see the problem overcome.

Time brought solutions, and there would be popular Virginia wineries in the 1800s, among them Monticello Wine Company and Garrett & Company, but the state did not enter into its own wine production until the 1970s. Today, the Old Dominion produces world-class vintages—Viognier and red blends are especially of note—from some three hundred wineries.

Raise a Glass: Cider and Brandy Drinks

In addition to beer and wine, Virginians also began crafting drinks from fruits that were available—such as apples, berries, paw-paws, peaches and pears—to make brandy or cider. Some fruits, like apples, were not native to North America (although the crabapple is), but they started arriving in the New World around the first quarter of the seventeenth century.

Note that all alcoholic drinks are fermented, but not all are distilled. While fermentation can happen by accident (and does so in nature), distillation takes additional equipment and skill to purify—and, as such, additional expense. But to craft a drink such as cider, it mostly takes a food that has a sugar content and time. Like using the juice of grapes to make wine, cider takes the juice of apples and the like, as well as bacteria and yeast feed from the natural sweetness, adding alcohol and usually a bit of effervescence.

Apples and cider-making continues to be a rich part of Virginia heritage; the state is the sixth-largest apple producing state by acreage in the United

States, and Virginia Cider Week is set aside for celebration each November. Today, there are more than twenty cideries across the Commonwealth.

In *A Perfect Description of Virginia*, the author noted:

> *Mr. Richard Bennet had this yeer out of his Orchard as many Apples as he made 20 Butts of excellent Cider.*
>
> *And Mr. Richard Kinsman hath had for this three or four yeers, forty or fifty Butts of Perry* [pear cider] *made out of his Orchard, pure and good.*
>
> *So that you may perceive how proper our Country is for these fruits, and men begin now to plant great Orchards, and find the way of Grafting upon Crab-stocks, best for lasting, here being naturally in this Land store of wild Crab-trees. Mr. Hough at Nausamund, hath a curious Orchard also, with all kind and variety of several fruits; the Governour in his new Orchard hath 15 hundred fruit-trees, besides his Apricocks, Peaches, Mellicotons, Quinces, Wardens, and such like fruits. I mention these particular men, that all may know the truth of things.*

Also noted in this work is the establishment of honey bees, instrumental in orchard development and introduced by Europeans in the early seventeenth century: "For Bees there is in the Country which thrive and prosper very well there: one Mr. George Pelton, alias, Strayton, a ancient planter of twenty-five yeers standing that had store of them, he made thirty pounds a yeer profit of them…he makes excellent good Matheglin, a pleasant and strong drink, and it serves him and his family for good liquor." Note that matheglin is a spiced type of mead, a honey wine.

Distillation takes fermentation a bit further, and because additional steps and purification occur, distilled spirits store longer than fermented drink—plus, because of their concentration of alcohol, they pack more of a punch. Brandies, such as peach brandy, became popular distilled fruit–based drinks. A Virginia specialty became applejack, an amber spirit with a deep, rich smoothness.

Like with beer, many folks made these drinks at home, crafting just enough for their use or maybe producing a little extra to sell. As taverns began to emerge, innkeepers would also often produce their own or purchase from within the community.

According to the folks at Mount Vernon, George Washington maintained orchards on his property, and ledgers in 1798 and 1799 note small productions of peach brandy. Some of this was used by Washington and his family at their Northern Virginia estate, while some was also sold at market. Today,

George Washington's Peach Brandy is distilled, aged and bottled by hand at George Washington's Distillery at Mount Vernon.

An advertisement from William D. Roberts Jr. in the *Norfolk and Portsmouth Phenix* newspaper on June 26, 1841, advertised brandy stills: "I have on hand Brandy Stills, 40, 80 and 120 gallons; Copper and Pewter Worms of all descriptions; and a large and general assortment of articles of TIN and COPPER MANUFACTURE.…Workmanship and material warranted. Old Stills repaired or taken in barter for new." An interesting note was that a prize of $100 was to "be awarded to the producer of a barrel of the best Apple Jack" using the stills.

RAISE A GLASS: DISTILLED SPIRITS

Distillation is a very specific process that occurs after fermentation and has its roots in science. Some primitive forms of distillation have been around since at least 1200 BC, when it was described in Babylonian tables, but the course taken today has only been around since medieval times.

It's through the actions of heating and cooling and collecting concentrated vapors that spirits such as gin, rum and whiskey occur. After the 1400s, specific formulas were being followed, and drinks like aquavit from the Scandinavians and genever from the Dutch emerged. Bushmills, the oldest whiskey still being distilled in the world, began in Ireland in 1608, the year following the First Landing.

John Smith mentioned in his *Generall Historie of Virginia* not just beer but sack (port wine) and aqua vitae in the possession of colony president Edward Wingfield. Aqua vitae, also spelled "aqua vita," comes from the Latin for "water of life" and was a term used from the Middle Ages on for a short period to describe many distilled spirits, including brandy.

Because of spotty records, and records lost over time, exactly who was distilling what and when in Jamestown is elusive. But excavations at the historic site have yielded some clues. One is of a building known as the Factory, located at the perimeter of a fort addition; it includes several artifacts, according to the folks at Historic Jamestowne, including "a glass alembic [a domed vessel used in distilling], a distilling flask, crucibles, and distilling dishes." The Factory, which included three brick hearths, was large enough to perhaps serve multiple purposes. Separate from the fort itself, it was also likely an outpost for trade.

In a well, a glass receiver, used in the distillation process, was also found nearly intact. Other excavations throughout the space revealed items such as a fine Chinese porcelain cup in a "flame frieze" decoration, which Historic Jamestowne noted was "probably used by the colony's gentlemen to drink their distilled spirits (aqua vitae)"; it was found in a circa 1610 part of James Fort.

This proves that the history of distilled spirits begins in Virginia, said Dr. William S. Dodson Jr., an owner of Eight Shires Coloniale Distillery in Williamsburg. "Currently, pieces of seven glass stills have been discovered in the remnants left at Jamestown settlement," he noted. Dodson added that, from measurements, five reproductions were made, with one at Historic Jamestowne and four being used in attempts to reproduce historic spirits at Eight Shires.

Dodson said that there have been other discoveries too, including ceramic stills excavated at Carter's Grove, near Jamestown. "The only remnants of commercial distillation in the Jamestown/Williamsburg time period are a round fireplace behind Marot's Tavern of a style similar to that used in Europe for distillation, but it is unknown if that was the actual use. Stills are documented in the transfer of ownership from Marot's to what is now known as Shield's Tavern."

From the mid-sixteenth century on, some plantation owners along the James River would import small distilleries from the Old World for personal use, according to Dodson.

Meet George Thorpe

George Thorpe was born at Wanswell Court, his family's Gloucestershire, England estate, and baptized on January 1, 1576. He likely studied law in London, married, was widowed and married again, having five children. Thorpe grew in prominence, holding post during a brief parliamentary session and becoming a major investor in several New World organizations, including the Virginia Company of London and Berkeley Hundred.

The Virginia Company of London, of course, was the joint stock venture set up in 1606 to establish colonial settlements in the New World. Berkeley Hundred was a settlement within the Colony of Virginia, located on the north bank of the James River between present-day Williamsburg and Richmond. The eight thousand acres later became known as Berkeley Plantation.

In 1618, Berkeley Hundred was established as a land grant by the Virginia Company of London to a group of men: Richard Berkeley, John Smyth, Sir William Throckmorton and Sir George Yeardley. Another in the group, The Society of Berkeley Hundred, was represented by Throckmorton's cousin

George Thorpe. The next year, about thirty-eight folks settled on the land, and with them on the ship *Margaret* were the supplies needed to get things started, including "[s]ome fifteen gallons of aqua vitae, five-and-a-half tuns of beer, and cider."

Thorpe arrived later, in 1620, and was appointed to the colony's Council of State, which advised the governor and performed judiciary duties. Thorpe was also put in charge of land set aside for a college and school for Native Americans to convert them to Christianity and establish them in English culture. He focused on the land, and on farming, even trying viticulture at one point by planting more than ten thousand grapevines, which failed.

The statesman was on a fast track to perhaps be governor himself one day. Then, on March 22, 1622, Thorpe, along with 346 other settlers at Berkeley and other plantations along the wandering James River, were attacked and killed by Native Americans, led by Opechancanough, at the beginning of the Anglo-Powhatan War. But it was twenty-nine words that Thorpe penned in a December 19, 1620 letter to John Smyth that truly cemented his place in history: "Wee have found a waie to make soe good drink of Indian corne I have divers times refused to drink good strong English beare and chose to drinke that."

What Thorpe most likely created was white dog, a clear, un-aged, raw whiskey that, with a little time in barrels, would turn golden and have its edge taken off. If it followed a specific protocol—according to the amount of corn in the mash, the type of barrel used for storage and not having any other additions—it could have been called bourbon. Of course, there are other names for the "corn beer" that Thorpe distilled in addition to "white dog," among them "white lightning," "white whiskey," "moonshine" and "hooch."

So, while not exactly bourbon, it was a good start to crafting truly American whiskeys in the developing nation. Virginia fostered this corn whiskey, and many farmers found that they could make about three gallons from a bushel of corn—the price they could fetch on their distilled spirits surpassed that of the corn at market. "The first corn liquor was thought to have its origins at Berkeley Plantation with the first documented use of American corn to make a 'beer,'" said Bill Dodson. "The leader of the settlement, Rev. George Thorpe, was known to be a distiller."

It would be more than a dozen years before a complete inventory on Thorpe's estate was crafted. "An Inventorie of All and Singular the Goods and Effectes of Captayne George Thorpe. Esquire Deceased, Valued and

This postcard depicts planting corn at the Jamestown Settlement. Corn would have been used for beer, food and spirits. *Author's collection.*

Prised the 10th Day of Aprill Anno 1634 by Samuell Sharpe, Richard Biggs and Thomas Palmer" seems to confirm Thorpe's interest and engagement in distilling. One item was "item copper still, old," and was valued at three pounds of tobacco. An equally interesting note is this: "Item a small runlett of Rosasolus and 3 runs. of Virginia, which were drunke out amonge the people that fetcht downe his goods."

A runlett, runlet or run is an archaic term for a cask of beer, wine or other drink. Rosasolus or Rosa Solis was a popular cordial water of the time, a type of forerunner to modern-day liqueurs. Golden in color, rosasolus was crafted with the bog plant sundew and a number of spices and other ingredients and then consumed as an aphrodisiac and for other health reasons. Sometimes small amounts of edible flecks of gold leaf were added for special effect.

But the truly intriguing part of the note is the "3 runs. of Virginia" that were drunk, and presumably enjoyed, by Sharpe, Biggs, Palmer and others inventorying his goods. Sitting in casks for all those years, it is probable that this was the aged corn beer, or whiskey, that Thorpe had written to Smyth about.

In 2019, George Thorpe was inducted into the Virginia Culinary Hall of Fame.

The Rise of Taverns and Inns

Although there is some note of taverns in Jamestown, it wasn't until Virginia began to grow and expand, and until towns were established, that the need for them arose.

There were many names for these establishments, which largely mimicked what was found in England. Some were called taverns, others ordinaries and others still inns, but their core services were the same: provide a place to stop, grab an eat and drink and catch up on news. Some were bare-bones and basic, while others were more elaborate and expansive. The quality of food greatly varied—some taverns were noted for excellent fare, while others served up dishes that were barely edible.

As the colony expanded, they provided another function: a place for a traveler to spend the night. Roads were primitive, sometimes no more than an old Native American trail, and had to be traversed in all sorts of weather conditions. Early on, folks usually traveled on business; it was too dangerous and expensive to travel for leisure. Sometimes journeys would be by horse, often by foot. Farmers often used carts and wagons to transport goods. A ten-mile journey might require an overnight stay. Along these roads, taverns appeared to serve the traveling public needs.

Taverns also appeared in population-rich areas as new towns popped up. These towns began appearing with the establishment of plantations and tobacco warehouse centers as that cash crop grew. This shifted some tavern use then, from traveler to local, where folks would stop by for a tipple or two and to exchange ideas, information and news. By default, many taverns became clubhouses for those who frequented them. Later, it would be that exchange of ideas and information in taverns that germinated the seeds of disenchantment with Mother England, leading up to the Revolutionary War.

Many times, taverns were established next to courthouses, where folks would come from all over to conduct business. After a growth period, Virginia was divided in 1634 into eight shires, which began a division along the lines of what we now know as counties. The original eight shires were Accomack, Charles City, Charles River, Elizabeth City, Henrico, James City, Warrosquyoake and Warwick River.

As the colony's population grew, the shires expanded too, not only within the division of the original eight shires but with the formation of others as well, within and beyond the Coastal Virginia region. For travelers in a stagecoach rather than alone on horseback, the passage price often included food at stops at inns and/or taverns. Later, the name "inn" became more common for larger facilities that had a specific offering of lodging and not just eats and drinks. But regardless, the bill of fare at an ordinary, tavern or inn largely depended on what was available to the establishment owner.

Drinks were often served with meals, including ales or other styles of beer the tavern keepers crafted themselves; hard ciders crafted from what fruit was available were common too. Wine was popular, and early cocktails comprised rum by the drink or in punches or wine turned into sangrias or sangarees. What is known largely comes from advertisements, court records (legal actions, licensing) and diaries; they provide some information about what Virginians were eating and drinking in the seventeenth century, but information is spotty.

John Redwood operated perhaps the first tavern in Norfolk, establishing Redwood's Ordinary in 1693. Redwood and his family had been involved in the sugar/molasses/rum trade in Barbados when he received a grant for Lot 47 in downtown Norfolk. Supplementing a menu of food he was able to gather himself or procure from area farmers and watermen was a number of imbibes. At the time, the prices of beverages were regulated by the county court. According to Norfolk County records, patrons would have thrown back:

> *Rum, priced at 6 shillings per gallon*
> *Punch, "if made good," at 16 pence per quart*
> *Cider, 12 pence per gallon*
> *Small beer (a lower alcohol brew), 7-1/2 pence per gallon*
> *Madeira, 22-1/2 pence per quart*
> *Milk Punch, 7-1/2 pence per quart*
> *Claret, 3 shillings, 3-1/2 pence per quart*

It was also noted that meals cost three and three-fourths pence.

By the early part of the nineteenth century, true restaurants would emerge, and taverns and ordinaries would begin to more closely resemble the types of bars and other watering holes enjoyed today. (Notable, historic ordinaries, taverns and inns across Virginia still in operation today are listed in the "Resources" chapter.)

THE IMPORTANCE OF RUM

Virginia has had a long history with the Caribbean, even predating the establishment of the Jamestown colony.

During the historic first voyage of 1606–7, the ships *Susan Constant*, *Godspeed* and *Discovery* made port in several islands between their origin of London and their destination of Virginia. Well into their long, four-month journey, the three small ships sailed into the West Indies. Here they called on Martinique, Dominica, Guadalupe, St. Croix and Puerto Rico, picking up supplies before heading north.

They may have encountered sugar cane during their stops—cane fields and sugar mills were in the islands and South America as early as the first half of the sixteenth century. The canes, and the knowledge that they produced sugar, came from trade with Africa and had spread from other locations, including India and Asia, over time. In fact, in some of those areas, alcoholic beverages, including a sugar cane beer in India from around 1800 BC, were being made with the perennial tropical grass. Also, in the region of modern-day Iran, the explorer Marco Polo described in the fourteenth century a "very good wine of sugar."

But these were not rum. Sometime, perhaps in the mid-1500s or so in this region, someone made the first crude rum either with sugar cane juice or a byproduct from sugar processing, such as molasses, using a simple distilling technique. The result would have been harsh, but they likely saw the potential. It's possible that the idea simultaneously popped up at different locations around the same time, as the ingredients were available and the methods were known to many.

Rum was first documented in the British colony of Barbados in 1651 by a visitor, who reported, "The chief fuddling they make in the island is Rumbullion, alias Kill-Divil, and this is made of sugar canes distilled, a hot, hellish, and terrible liquor." The exact etymology for *rum* is lost, but we like the theory that it is linked to the word *rumbustious*.

Although historically this region had been a stronghold for the Spanish since Christopher Columbus laid claim in 1492, their influence was waning. The British, Dutch and French soon established a foothold. Bermuda, considered part of Virginia, was colonized by the British as early as 1612. Other islands followed suit, including a number of islands forming the British West Indies beginning in 1623. Barbados, where the first documentation of rum was noted, had particularly strong ties with Virginia; the island was colonized in 1627. In 1655, Jamaica was taken from the Spanish by the British.

This expansion was important because the Caribbean was a waypoint for many voyages from England on the way to Virginia; ships were laden with goods from both places and, often, slaves from Africa. Eventually, a triangular trade between these points was established, importing and exporting commodities along the way.

Slavery also included human trafficking in the Caribbean. Hard goods were often molasses, rum and sugar. Molasses and sugar had a number of uses, but foremost among those was the making of rum, particularly when rum crafted in the Caribbean was not purchased. Sugar cane was brought to Jamestown in 1619, but it did not grow; in the tropics, it took off like weeds. The importation of sugar from the British colonies in the Caribbean helped cut down the dependence on other sources under control of other nations. Sugar and molasses are, of course, used in edibles, but sugar is necessary for the production of rum, in which the cane is crushed and juice is extracted. One process in turning the sugar cane juice into rum is by turning the raw sugar into molasses; it is this method by which most rum is distilled.

Colonial Americans often picked rum as their drink of choice, although beer, brandies (made with any available fruit), ciders made from apples and pears, other spirits and wine (imported and made domestically from native grapes) were also enjoyed. Despite what was in their mug, Virginians were known to love their drink so much that as early as March 5, 1623, Governor Francis Wyatt and the colonial legislature declared Temperance Day, imposing fines on any colonist displaying public intoxication.

But the importance of rum—and thus the connection to the Caribbean—cannot be emphasized enough. According to A. Smith Bowman Distillery, which today crafts George Bowman Rum (a dark rum hand-bottled in Fredericksburg, Virginia), it is estimated that an average colonist quaffed three imperial gallons of rum annually. That's a staggering 308 shots per person, in addition to other alcoholic beverages consumed.

While rum crafted in the Caribbean was preferred, it was often cheaper and more available to get the spirit domestically distilled, hence the need for molasses and sugar. According to the Colonial Williamsburg Foundation, by 1770, there were more than 140 rum distilleries making about 4.8 million gallons annually across the colonies.

In the July 4, 1771 *Virginia Gazette*, it was advertised, "At our rum distillery here [in Norfolk] may be had a constant Supply of that Article, and Molosses, which we will sell on the lowest Terms. Those who favour us with their Orders may depend upon being well ____; and they will please to address them to Mr. William Calderbead, who conducts the business of the Distillery, or to Jamieson, Campbell, Calvert & Company"

The *Virginia Gazette* also ran an advertisement in its April 21, 1775 issue: "Roberdeau & Jackson Have for Sale at their new distillery, in the town of

Alexandria, on the river Potowmack, in the Colony of Virginia, ALEXANDRIA RUM, Which they engage equal in quality, either in strength, agreeable smell, and good flavour, to any made on this continent. They will be much obliged to the venders of that article for their custom, which they hope to merit, as well by the goodness of their rum, and the moderate profit they design to sell at, as their conitant endeavours to give general satisfaction. They propose to sell for cash only, or country produce delivered at the distillery."

An advertisement in the March 2, 1802 *Norfolk Herald* announced the opening of a new rum crafter, Gosport Distillery. Gosport is an area in Portsmouth. The ad read: "Manufacture of Rum, from Molasses; and the quantity already produced is deemed by Judges superior to that imported from the Northern States. The inhabitants of Norfolk are earnestly invited to a trial of its quality, and if they find it superior, or even equal to that which is imported, they respectfully solicit their patronage. It is now for sale at the store of Arch. Campbell, No. 112, Main-street, opposite Bank-street. William Atkinson & Co."

Folks were looking for accomplished distillers too. In the August 21, 1778 *Virginia Gazette*, it was advertised, "A man well acquainted with the business of DISTILLING will meet with immediate employment, by applying to me in Gloucester county. WARNER LEWIS."

In the hamlet of Manchester, now a neighborhood in Richmond, John Mayo published in the *Virginia Gazette* on December 19, 1777, the following: "Intending to set up a Brewery and Distillery at this Place. I have provided two Stills and three Coppers, one of which contains about 300 Gallons. The Situation and Convenience for carrying on that Business at this Place are equal to any. A person properly qualified, by Experience, to superintend such Business, may become a Partner, by applying shortly."

Ezekiel Hendrick tooted his own horn in the *Virginia Gazette* in November 28, 1777, advertising: "I do hereby inform the publick, that I have taken the greatest care to acquaint myself with the DISTILLING BUSINESS, and can undertake to make two gallons and a half of good spirit from every bushel of good wheat. Any person inclining to be perfected in the business may apply to me in Prince Edward county."

What's interesting about the advertisements for the search for the distillers in Gloucester and Richmond is that the type of spirit is not mentioned, and with the post from Ezekiel Hendrick, the spirit mentioned is not rum but whiskey.

Sugar would continue to be an important commodity. In the eighteenth century, the Sugar Act of 1764 was levied on the colonies as a tariff on molasses and sugar (and other shipped goods) from countries other than Great Britain, notably France and Spain's interests in the West Indies. It was done to increase revenue to pay down British debt but hit during a time of economic depression. The Sugar Act is cited as one of the factors that led to unrest in America leading up to the Revolutionary War. Also, cost and irregular availability of rum began to turn the nation more toward whiskey drinking, which could be made easily enough with corn and rye.

In the October 17, 1862 edition of the *Alexandria Gazette*, an unnamed writer opined on "Popular Drinks" in Virginia: "In 'ye olden times,' Jamaica rum was a favorite 'drink' in Virginia, and the flavor of aromatic punches seems still to linger 'round many of the ancient homesteads."

Interestingly, in 1832, "the use of rum as a beverage, for reasons unknown to the writer, was generally discontinued, and only thought of at Christmas when it became necessary to flavor egg-nogg." The writer speculates that the increased popularity of mint juleps and smashes made with brandy may have had something to do with it. But perhaps the seeds were established with the Sugar Act.

RECIPES

BUMBO

There were plenty of unusual-sounding drinks during the seventeenth and eighteenth centuries, including bogus, blackstrap, bombo, flip, mimbo, rattle skull, sling, syllabub, whistle belly, stone wall and toddy. And then there was bumbo, also called bumboo or bombo, a drink related to the traitor.

Bumbo was a favorite in the pirate-era Caribbean. Think of it as an upgrade to the navy's grog. The simple but potent drink was often used to favor friends, especially during election. One point in fact: in July 1758, George Washington treated voters during his campaign for the Virginia House of Burgesses to the cocktail, with documents noting that he used 160 gallons of rum in the process.

2 ounces dark or spiced rum
1 ounce fresh lemon or lime juice
½ teaspoon grenadine or raspberry syrup
¼ teaspoon freshly grated nutmeg

In a shaker filed with ice, add rum, citrus juice, grenadine (or raspberry syrup) and nutmeg. Shake well. Strain into a martini glass. Garnish with freshly grated nutmeg. Yields 1 cocktail.

FLIP

A late seventeenth-century drink, flip was a heady mixture of beer, rum, molasses, eggs and other ingredients. Traditionally, the imbibe was created by placing the ingredients in a pitcher and the tavern keeper thrusting a red-hot poker—referred to as a flip-dog—from the fireplace into it, stirring it up and whipping it into a froth while heating it through and pouring it into mugs for folks to enjoy.

2 beaten eggs
2 ounces rum
2 tablespoons brown sugar or molasses
12 ounces brown ale
¼ teaspoon cinnamon
freshly grated nutmeg

In a mug/tankard or heat-safe pint glass, add beaten eggs (or two or three ounces of heavy cream) with rum and brown sugar or molasses. In a small saucepan, heat a brown ale or other flavorful beer over low. Add cinnamon and stir occasionally; do not bring to a boil. When beer is heated and begins to steam, slowly pour into the mug/tankard and do so back and forth several times to temper so that the eggs or cream don't curdle. Garnish with nutmeg.
Yields 1 cocktail.

GROG

Rum was already a well-established drink in the New World by the end of the seventeenth century. Throughout Virginia and the other colonies, and across the Caribbean, it was often the beverage of choice. In 1655, after England conquered Jamaica, rum was distributed to sailors as part of their rations.

Grog—made with rum, water and other ingredients—comes from the nickname for British admiral Edward Vernon, who, in 1740, cut sailors' daily rations of rum with water while in command in the West Indies. Why was he called "Old Grog"? Vernon was noted for wearing a coat make of grogram cloth. Groggy means sleepy, such as when too much grog is consumed.

Dispensing grog to sailors became a tradition that transferred to the Continental navy and to the U.S. Navy as well. Anchors aweigh.

Honey Syrup
1 cup honey
1 cup water

Cocktail
1 ½ ounces dark or spiced rum
1 ½ ounces white rum
1 ounce fresh lime juice
1 ounce honey syrup
soda water
lime wedge

To make the honey syrup, in a small saucepan add honey and water and bring to a boil, stirring frequently. Reduce to a simmer and stir frequently until honey has dissolved. Remove from stove and cool. Add to a sealable glass jar and refrigerate until use, up to 1 month.

To make the cocktail, in a shaker filled with ice add dark rum, white rum, lime juice and honey syrup; cover; and shake vigorously. Strain into a tall glass with ice and fill with soda water. Garnish with lime wedge. Yields 1 cocktail.

MADE-GOOD PUNCH

John Redwood operated perhaps the first tavern in Norfolk, establishing Redwood's Ordinary in 1693. Redwood and his family had been involved in the sugar/molasses/rum trade in Barbados when he received a grant for Lot 47 in downtown Norfolk. Supplementing a menu of what food he was able to gather himself or procure from area farmers and watermen, was a number of imbibes.

Among the offering was "Punch, if made good" at sixteen pence per quart, as regulated by the Norfolk County court. Punches, in general, were very popular in Colonial Virginia. They were boozy and ubiquitous in the colony. "Punch was the gentleman's drink," said Master of Historic Foodways at Colonial Williamsburg Frank Clark. "It was used as a social lubricant and to finalize business deals."

We don't know what John Redwood crafted, but our punch recipe is inspired by punches of the time using guidelines provided by Clark.

Ginger Simple Syrup
1 3-inch piece fresh ginger
1 cup sugar
1 cup water

Cocktail
2 cups spiced rum
1 cup fresh squeezed lime juice
1 cup fresh squeezed lemon juice
1 cup fresh squeezed orange juice
1 cup ginger simple syrup
sparkling water
freshly grated nutmeg

Make the simple syrup by peeling the skin from the piece of ginger and slicing into thin disks. In a small saucepan over medium-high heat, add the ginger, sugar and water and bring to a boil, stirring occasionally, until sugar is dissolved. Remove from heat and allow to cool to room temperature. Strain, add to a sealable glass jar and refrigerate until use, up to 1 month.

In a punch bowl, add the rum, lime juice, lemon juice, orange juice and ginger simple syrup. Serve half a cup of punch, top with sparkling water and garnish with freshly grated nutmeg.
Yields 12–16 cocktails.

MILK PUNCH

"The English had a long tradition of mixing alcohol and milk to create a variety of foodstuffs," noted Frank Clark. One of the most popular of these during the colonial period was syllabub; another was posset. Then there was milk punch, a highly spirited mixture of milk, sugar, vanilla extract and a spirit, be it brandy, rum or whiskey. Akin to eggnog, milk punch is served cold, typically in a punch bowl, and individual cups are usually garnished with nutmeg atop.

Milk punch was first written about in the latter part of the seventeenth century in Europe and, within a few years, had obviously become well known and enjoyed. It was on John Redwood's tavern's bill of fare in Norfolk in 1693, selling for seven and a half pence per quart.

Simple Syrup
1 cup sugar
1 cup water

Cocktail
3 ounces milk
1 ½ ounces spiced rum
¾ ounce simple syrup
¼ teaspoon pure vanilla extract
freshly grated nutmeg
cinnamon stick

Make the simple syrup by adding the sugar and water to a small saucepan over medium-high heat and bringing to a boil, stirring occasionally, until sugar is dissolved. Remove from heat and allow to cool to room temperature. Add to a sealable glass jar and refrigerate until use, up to 1 month.

In a cocktail shaker filled with ice, add milk, spiced rum, simple syrup and vanilla extract and shake vigorously until drink is chilled. Strain into a Collins or martini glass and garnish with freshly grated nutmeg and a cinnamon stick. Yields 1 cocktail.

RATTLE-SKULL

This popular colonial-era cocktail does just as the name implies—it rattles the skull after enjoying a few of these boozy imbibes, although rattle-skull is actually an English colloquialism for someone who chats, or rattles on, too much.

You can use a brown ale of choice in this drink, but based on patriotism, we recommend an American porter, which is noted as George Washington's favorite brew. In a letter written on January 29, 1789, to the Marquis de Lafayette from his Mount Vernon home, the president wrote about his eat-and-drink America first policy: "We have already been too long subject to British prejudices. I use no porter or cheese in my family, but such as is made in America; both these articles may now be purchased of an excellent quality." Washington in particular seemed to favor the porters of Robert Hare and Benjamin Wistar Morris, both brewers in Philadelphia.

Brown Sugar Syrup
1 cup dark brown sugar, lightly packed
1 cup water

Cocktail
2½ ounces dark or spiced rum
½ ounce fresh lime juice
½ ounce brown sugar simple syrup
12 ounces porter or brown ale
freshly grated nutmeg

For the brown sugar simple syrup, in a small saucepan over medium-high heat add the brown sugar and water and bring to a boil, stirring occasionally until sugar is dissolved. Remove from heat and allow to cool to room temperature. Add to a sealable glass jar and refrigerate until use, up to 1 month.

For the cocktail, in a chilled pint glass, add rum, lime juice and simple syrup and stir. Add porter and garnish with freshly grated nutmeg. Yields 1 cocktail.

STRAWBERRY SHRUB

Shrubs began in England as a medieval cordial water or liqueur with medicinal purposes and shifted in style and purpose in Colonial America. Fruit vinegars give the drink a punch, as well as a fresh flavor when citrus may not be available. Shrubs were consumed on their own or often used as a base for punches.

Our recipe uses strawberries; on April 26, 1607, the first settlers began to explore the land, finding many wonderful things to eat, including strawberries. In writings from historian George Percy, who was with Captain John Smith during his travels, he noted exploring the area around the Lynnhaven River in present-day Virginia Beach: "Going a little further we came into a plat of ground full of fine and beautifull Strawberries, foure times bigger and better than ours in England." Berries grew wild in Virginia Beach and throughout the region; the area in Hampton known today as Strawberry Banks was noted in 1619 by John Smith for the abundance of the fruit there.

In addition to strawberries, you could use a similar amount of other berries or other fruit. While the spirit used in this recipe is rum, you can use sherry or another alcohol such as vodka. You can make a non-alcoholic drink by increasing the amount of sparkling water.

Shrub
1 cup water
1 cup sugar
4 cups hulled and quartered strawberries
1 cup white wine vinegar

Cocktail
2 ounces rum
4 ounces sparkling water

To make the shrub, combine the water and sugar in a medium saucepan over medium heat and bring to a boil, stirring constantly until the sugar dissolves. Reduce the heat to medium-low, add the strawberries and simmer until thickened, 10 to 15 minutes, stirring occasionally and lightly mashing the fruit against the side of the saucepan. Remove the mixture from the heat and let cool for 15 to 20 minutes. Strain the liquid into a sealable, quart-sized glass jar, pressing the strawberry solids to extract as much juice as possible. Discard the strawberries. Add the vinegar to the jar, stir and refrigerate until chilled, at least 1 hour.

To make the cocktail, stir 1 ounce of the shrub base and the rum together in a tall glass. Fill the glass with ice, pour in the sparkling water and stir to incorporate. Serve immediately. Yields 1 cocktail.

STONE FENCE

This classic colonial cocktail combines a number of Virginia's culinary calling cards, among them hard cider and rum, and showcases the flavors of fall.

Virginia knows apples—more than one hundred commercial orchards cover some sixteen thousand acres of land in the state, producing 5 to 6 million bushels annually. The Shenandoah Valley is apple country, although many of the dozen or so varieties grown here also come from the Roanoke Valley as well as Albemarle, Carroll, Patrick and Rappahannock Counties. The region's favorite fruit is celebrated each spring with the Shenandoah Apple Blossom Festival, held since 1924 in Winchester. The six-day festival—which features a carnival, concerts and a parade—sees the town's population of 24,000 swell to more than 250,000.

Apple cider is celebrated with its own official week each November; for this recipe, we are partial to Richmond's Blue Bee Cider. (Also of note: Virginia is the southernmost state where maple syrup is produced, with an annual Maple Festival held each spring in remote Highland County along the Eastern Continental Divide in the Allegheny Mountains.)

4 ounces hard cider
2 ounces spiced rum
1 ounce pure maple syrup or simple syrup
2–3 dashes Angostura or orange bitters

In a highball glass, add cider, rum, syrup and bitters and stir. Add ice and serve. Yields 1 cocktail.

RUM BALLS

Rum balls are an old-timey treat, especially around the holidays. These easy-to-craft confections bring together a number of complementary tastes and textures, including a good dose of spiced rum, such as the author's Four Farthing Spiced Rum. The secret is to make the rum balls at least one day before you serve them or give them away as a gift to allow time for all the flavors to marry.

1 12-ounce box (2½ cups) vanilla wafer crumbs
1 cup finely chopped, toasted pecans
1¾ cups confectioners' sugar
2 tablespoons unsweetened cocoa powder
2½ tablespoons light corn syrup
½ cup spiced rum

In a large bowl, combine vanilla wafers, pecans, 1 cup confectioners' sugar and cocoa; stir to incorporate. In a small bowl, whisk corn syrup and spiced rum and pour over vanilla wafers mix, then stir well to completely incorporate. Place in refrigerator for 5 minutes.

In a large bowl, place ¾ cup confectioners' sugar. Remove vanilla wafer/bourbon mixture and, using a melon scoop, scoop out balls and roll in confectioners' sugar. Place in an airtight container in the refrigerator at least 1 day before serving to allow flavors to meld. Roll in additional confections sugar before service. Will keep in an airtight container for 2–3 weeks. Yields about 4 dozen balls.

Chapter 2

THE EIGHTEENTH CENTURY

WESTWARD, HO!

The Virginia that was established at the beginning of the seventeenth century was not the same Virginia that was ending it.

In 1607, three small ships with a bit more than one hundred men and boys made their way from England across the Atlantic Ocean as part of a commercial enterprise, the Virginia Company. And all along, the Virginia Company wanted one thing and one thing only: to set up a permanent settlement in the New World and to turn a profit doing it.

There were several ways the Virginia Company hoped to pay back its investors and turn a tidy sum of its own. First was looking for raw materials, like gold and silver, and also glass, sassafras, tar and timber. The second was to produce certain goods—a number of artisans and craftsmen made the trip—cheaper than they could in England and ship them back. Other schemes included producing wine at the same quality as France and setting up silkworm production to rival China.

Another reason: the fabled Northwest Passage. The Virginia Company was but one of many concerns that wanted to find a shortcut from Europe to the rich trade economy in Asia by heading northwest, rather than arduously around the cape of Africa. As it was written in the 1606 document "Instructions from the Virginia Company of London to the First Settlers":

You must Observe if you Can Whether the River on which You Plant Doth Spring out of Mountains or out of Lakes if it be out of any Lake the passage to the Other Sea will be the more Easy and it is Like Enough that Out of the same Lake you shall find Some Spring which run the Contrary way toward the East India Sea for the Great and famous River of Volga Tan[a]is and Dwina have three heads near joynd and Yet the One falleth into the Caspian Sea the Other into the Euxine Sea and the third into the Polonian Sea.

So, as the men and boys toiled under the hot Virginia sun, raising a fort at Jamestown in the unforgiving heat near the stagnant, mosquito-infested waters, it was understood that this tiny space of about one acre, surrounded by piked logs driven into the grounds protecting the handful of colonists, was just the beginning.

Within a few years, other forts and settlements around there were being established; Hampton, founded in 1610, today remains the oldest English-speaking city in North America. But most of the growth was north and west. Once tobacco was discovered to be the valuable commodity the Virginia Company was looking for, a boom in 1620 pushed settlements up the James River to present-day Richmond. The colony's population was about 400, according to the U.S. Census. The colony's capital moved from Jamestown to Williamsburg in 1699 as the population of Virginia swelled to about 58,000. A century later, the population would be around 800,000.

Movement west continued because of the promise of riches—not for the Virginia Company now, but for Mother England herself, for the Old Dominion had become a Crown Colony in 1660. Many also did it for themselves. Sporadic exploration of the area west of the James River fall line occurred early on, but perhaps one of the most noted expeditions was the Knights of the Golden Horseshoe Expedition. This expedition's participants received gold horseshoe pins. This trip was led in 1716 by Governor Alexander Spotswood. The party marched into the wilderness—lands seen by few, if any Europeans. They spied the dusky Blue Ridge Mountains and made their way into the reaches of the fabled Shenandoah, which charming legend says translates to "beautiful daughter of the stars."

They looked up and down the valley at the river that cuts up its center and laid claim in the name of King George I. They then celebrated as follows, according to diarist John Fontaine:

We drank the King's health in champagne and fired a volley, the Princess's health in Burgundy and fired a volley, and all the rest of the royal family in claret and a volley. We drank the Governor's health and fired another volley. We had several sorts of liquors, viz: Virginia red wine and white wine, Irish usquebaugh [whiskey], *brandy, shrub, two sorts of rum, champagne, canary, cherry punch, cider, &c.*

The possibilities seemed endless. Perhaps the Pacific lay just over the next ridge. Maybe there was gold here. Perhaps this was a good place to grow tobacco or maybe corn. But today, the real riches are in the description of what sounds like quite the celebration. The list of alcoholic beverages enjoyed is like a who's who: Burgundy wine and claret, another red wine, to start, as well as mention of Virginia red and white wines, shrub, champagne, canary (a fortified wine) and cider. On the list too were "several sorts of liquors"—perhaps some distilled in Virginia? Also on the list were Irish whiskey, brandy and not one but *two* sorts of rum. To round things out, there was a cherry punch, no doubt highly strengthened with booze of some sort.

During the eighteenth century, folks moved westward for a number of reasons. One was for more opportunity to farm. For about one hundred years or so, the eastern part of the state had been heavily farmed for tobacco, which is hard on the soil, depleting many nutrients. Some farmers moved out west to look for new large tracts of land to farm.

Another is that many were finishing up their contract time as indentured servants, and they began acquiring land of their own. Because land in the East was established and valuable, the more affordable option was to move where there was more land available, and that was west of Coastal Virginia. Others still received land grants and moved because of the promise of opportunities.

There was also a sense of freedom in the West that didn't necessarily exist in the East, particularly for certain classes of folks. As the population moved into the Piedmont, over in the Shenandoah Valley, nestled in the hollers of the Allegheny and Blue Ridge Mountains and down into the Roanoke Valley, a more greater sense of equality was coming about. Most settlers, including the arriving Scotch-Irish, lived a hardscrabble life. Out here, on the frontier, they were away from many of the large plantations and plantation owners who, due to their social stature and wealth, had great influence in the community.

The Scotch-Irish were a group that settled into the western part of Virginia. They came from Ulster in Northern Ireland starting in 1715. But they came not from Coastal Virginia and the East, but rather largely from the port of Philadelphia and down the Great Wagon Road. Some stayed in

OLD TAVERN.

A tavern in the Shenandoah Valley in the late 1700s, from *Stories of the Old Dominion*, 1879. *Author's collection.*

Virginia, bringing their culture, including their ways of distillation, while others moved farther west, through the Cumberland Gap to lands beyond the horizon.

Perhaps the Scotch-Irish, once settled in, made up a batch of usquebaugh, their unique style of whiskey, as noted in the diary of John Fontaine on that famed 1716 expedition by Governor Alexander Spotswood.

Another immigrant group moving into areas west of the larger settlements along the coast of Virginia were the Germans. In 1714 and 1717, Virginia lieutenant governor Alexander Spotswood encouraged miners from Germany to move to the colony to establish a mining industry here. The settlement of Germanna was established near Culpepper, with folks also bringing their culture to the melting pot, such as methods of crafting spirits, maybe a schnapps or other strong cordial.

Others came too—some on their own, like French Huguenots and Welsh, while others, such as enslaved Africans, were brought by force. Across an ever-increasing size of land, they all contributed their concept of eats and drinks.

Virginia eventually held claim to lands stretching well beyond the current borders. Parts of Illinois, Indiana and Ohio were carved from land ceded by Virginia in 1784, as well as Kentucky in 1792. West Virginia separated from Virginia in 1862.

The isolation and remoteness of all of this land helped fuel an emerging Virginia economic engine: whiskey.

VIRGINIA: THE BIRTHPLACE OF THE AMERICAN SPIRIT

For a good part of the 1700s, rum continued to be the drink of choice for many Virginians—in fact, for most colonists across British America.

In Virginia, wharfs from the Tidewater of the state up the Chesapeake Bay and its tributaries unloaded barrels full of fine rum from Barbados, Jamaica and other ports of call across the Caribbean, as well as raw materials for distilling rum here, such as sugar and molasses, should you choose. Many did choose: Colonial Williamsburg noted that by 1770, there were more than 140 rum distilleries, producing some 4.8 million gallons annually across the colonies.

That's not to say that the eighteenth-century Virginian drank nothing but rum. Beer was still an overwhelming favorite alcoholic drink, as were wines made from grapes and other fruits. There were brandies, sherries and canaries, as well as other distilled and fortified wines. Some of the London Gin Craze of the midcentury spilled over across the Pond. And you can't leave out Irish whiskies, aqua vitae, syrupy cordials and liqueurs and other intoxicating liquids to make the spirit bright.

But several factors began shifting during this period that turned America's favorite hard drink away from rum and toward whiskey. One large factor had to do with what was available to distill. As settlers moved farther away from Coastal Virginia and its ports, the transportation of heavy barrels full of commodities—in this case either rum itself or its chief ingredients in production, sugar and/or molasses—made the trek either difficult or impossible. Folks who were several days away from cities like Alexandria, Richmond or Norfolk had to be as self-sufficient as possible, even more so if they were over the Blue Ridge Mountains and into the Shenandoah Valley or beyond.

But here corn—and other grains—grew abundantly, and it was corn that was used to create a spirit, whiskey, for drinking. This was how it had been more than a century before in 1620 when George Thorpe distilled his corn beer.

Speaking of beer, even though it was brewed and enjoyed, folks living the rough-and-tumble life on the frontier saw the practical benefits of spirits,

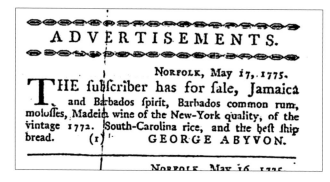

A May 17, 1775 *Virginia Gazette* advertisement announcing Barbados rum and molasses, among other goods, arriving in Norfolk from Jamaica. *Author's collection.*

which could be distilled and then stored for long periods of time—practically indefinitely. Beer did not have the same longevity.

By distilling the corn into whiskey, another problem was solved: easily transporting harvested crops to market. At harvest time, getting wagons loaded down with corn, other grains and other offerings through narrow, sometimes virtually nonexistent roads through passages and sometimes across mountains to towns to sell was tricky at best. It was easier to distill the corn, rye and the like and have a more concentrated—and profitable—item to haul and merchandise. The whiskey was also less likely to spoil in storage, transportation and distribution than the raw grain itself.

Another factor was the influence of the Scotch-Irish and their tradition of whisky (Americans added the *e* in *whiskey*) production, which had gone back several hundred years at this point. In fact, the Old Bushmills Distillery was licensed in Ireland in 1608, making it the oldest licensed whiskey distillery in the world. The migrants brought with them many traditions, including their craft of distilling. Like settlers before them, they adapted use with what they had. Instead of utilizing barley and other grains they had used in Europe, they followed their Virginia neighbors' leads and made use of corn. They also distilled rye, a type of grass.

The stills the Scotch-Irish set up in the mountains of Virginia—following their generations of distilling techniques but marrying that with styles already established here, as well as the grains grown in the Old Dominion—produced unaged whiskeys that would be highly lauded for generations.

And if you didn't run a still yourself while traversing through the backcountry of Virginia, a drink was never far. "The Wilderness Road, the northern route over the Alleghenies from Virginia, had whiskey for sale at strategic points along its length when it was little more than a path through the forests," wrote Iain Gately in his book *Drink: A Cultural History of Alcohol.*

Gately also noted a 1775 diary entry by Virginian William Calk as he was moving westward: "Wedn. 22nd we Start early and git to foart Chissel whear we git Some good loaf Bread & good Whiskey."

As tensions between the American colonies and England increased, rum imports and rum production decreased, while production of whiskey with local ingredients increased. British actions increasingly made getting rum, sugar and molasses from the Caribbean more difficult, expensive and sporadic. And that was before the Sugar Act of 1764 (which modified the earlier Molasses Act) was levied on the colonies.

This was a tariff on molasses and sugar (and other shipped goods) from countries other than Great Britain, notably France and Spain's interests in the West Indies. It was done to increase revenue to pay down British debt but hit during a time of economic depression. The Sugar Act is cited as one of the factors that led to unrest in America leading up to the Revolutionary War.

Then there was the war itself. Comestibles were on the frontline in many cases; colonists eschewed tea, seeing it as a symbol of Britain, and they moved away from the hot drink in favor of another: coffee. The same, to an extent, held true with rum. Although folks didn't flee to the nearest harbor and dump it in, all of a sudden there was a sense of patriotism when drinking whiskey crafted in the colonies—the true American spirit.

A May 24, 1766 *Virginia Gazette* advertisement announcing West India rum, sugar and other goods arriving in Norfolk from the Caribbean. *Author's collection.*

So, it wasn't just in the West that whiskey was gaining in popularity. Several advertisements in the *Virginia Gazette* of the time noted its sale, such as this post from Yorktown shop keep James Smith on December 27, 1776, listing it equally with other spirits and commodities: "For SALE, at my store in York town, WEST INDIA and New England rum, Madeira wine, peach brandy, whisky, lump and powdered sugar, allspice, ginger, nutmegs, coffe, tea."

REVOLUTION

With fires fueled for revolution in America's inns, ordinaries and taverns over tankards filled with whiskey and other spirits distilled in the colonies, the formal revolt against England launched in 1765, ending with the surrender of the British army under General Cornwallis at Yorktown in 1781. The American Revolution led to the freedom of the colonies and independence for the fledgling nation.

The Declaration of Independence was adopted by the Continental Congress on July 4, 1776, signed by fifty-six members, including seven Virginians: Carter Braxton, Benjamin Harrison V, Thomas Jefferson, Francis Lightfoot Lee, Richard Henry Lee, Thomas Nelson Jr. and George Wythe.

During the time at war, citizens and soldiers were affected in many ways as battles were fought on American soil. Men and boys went off to fight, and supplies were either rationed or hard to come by otherwise. The economy suffered. On the battlefield, a typical supply of food and drink issued by George Washington to his troops in 1778 included small amounts of beef or fish, pork, flour or bread, peas or beans and "one gill of whiskey or spirits," according to Charles Knowles Bolton in his book *The Private Soldier Under Washington*. The estimated cost was about eleven cents per soldier; one gill is equivalent to four ounces. "When the army was in camp a market was

Raleigh Tavern, Williamsburg, circa 1940. *Author's collection.*

established, where farmers were allowed to offer their produce for sale; and one suttling booth was permitted within each brigade's limits where liquor might be sold at fixed prices," noted Bolton.

Later, the ration was reduced to two ounces of whiskey or spirits in 1790 but doubled in 1794 for troops in combat or in service in the frontier. The double ration was extended in 1799 for troops engaged in fatigue duties, such as labor done without the use of armament. The rations would change again in the next century.

In an August 1777 letter penned by George Washington to John Hancock, the general noted that the "benefits arising from the moderate use of strong Liquor have been experienced in all Armies and are not to be disputed."

On the homefront, the American Revolution affected not only many lives but also many spirits. "The Revolution meant the decline of rum and the ascendancy of whiskey in America," wrote Mary Miley Theobald in "When Whiskey Was the King of Drink" for Colonial Williamsburg. "When the British blockade of American ports cut off the molasses trade, most New England rum distillers converted to whiskey. Whiskey had a patriotic flavor. It was an all-American drink, made in America by Americans from American grain, unlike rum, wine, gin, Madeira, brandy, coffee, chocolate, or tea, which had to be imported and were taxed."

MEET ELIJAH CRAIG

There's an old joke that goes, "How many Virginians does it take to change a lightbulb?" The answer is three: one to change the bulb and two to talk about how good the old bulb was. Virginians love their place in history, even if some of the legend and lore is muddled a bit through time and tippling. But often there is just enough truth to make a story compelling.

The truth is that the Old Dominion already has a long, documented history of distilling corn into liquor, as noted by the letters of George Thorpe at Berkeley Plantation in 1620 as the seventeenth century rolled along. With the introduction of old-world techniques mastered by the Scotch-Irish immigrants and a century of practice, Virginians knew their way around a still even by the time a man named Elijah Craig was born in the rolling Piedmont countryside of Orange County. Since at least 1874, Craig has been called the Father of Bourbon; even the spirits crafted today in his name by Heaven Hills Brands, located in Kentucky, proclaim it to be true on each bottle.

Of note: all bourbon is whiskey, but not all whiskey is bourbon. What is it that Craig, or a contemporary of his distilling spirits about this time, did that made that leap? In order for a whiskey to be called bourbon, it must be made from a mash that is at least 51 percent corn and aged—for no particular amount of time—in new, charred oak barrels. The "corn beer" distilled by George Thorpe in 1620 was a predecessor to modern-day bourbon because it was not added to new, charred oak barrels.

Like countless others, Craig moved west. In 1782, immediately after the American Revolution, Craig, by then a Baptist preacher, headed to Kentucky County in Virginia. He established a classical school and built mills for cloth, lumber and rope manufacturing/processing. He served as fire chief. In 1789, a good three years before Kentucky broke away from Virginia and became its own state, the entrepreneur founded a distillery.

It was here that Craig is said to have added his whiskey to some charred oak barrels, which, after some time, imparted a unique color and taste. And why were the barrels charred? The exact answer isn't known, although it may have started as a byproduct of the coopering process. It's noted that French cognac distillers would also char barrels in which to store their cognac. It's also noted that folks often burned out the interior of barrels as a way of removing leftover remnants of what was stored in it before, an elementary way of sanitizing so the costly vessel could be used again.

Regardless, as the 1700s were drawing to a close, bourbon was emerging, with the name associated with the Virginia county (later Kentucky) where the practice originated—or so goes the lore and legend.

Elijah Craig died in 1808.

GEORGE WASHINGTON, MASTER DISTILLER

'Tis Washington's health—fill a bumper all round,
For he is our glory and pride.
Our arms shall in battle with conquest be crown'd
Whilst virtue and he's on our side.
—a toast to General Washington, 1788

Many folks know George Washington as an important general who led the Continental army to victory over the British during the American Revolutionary War and as the United States' first president. The farmer and statesman, born in 1732 in Westmoreland County, has one more accolade to add: distiller.

Throughout his life, George Washington enjoyed alcoholic beverages, but he wasn't known to overindulge. On a trip to the Allegheny Mountains in 1784, he filled his canteen with cherry bounce. George Washington's Mount Vernon notes that beer was his favorite drink, particularly a porter. At night, after dinner, he might sip on a glass of Madeira.

But there were other times he let down his powdered wig. When George Washington first ran for elected office in 1755 at age twenty-three for a seat to the Virginia House of Burgesses, he came in with a disappointing 6.88 percent of the votes in Frederick County, which he hoped to represent. But three years later, when he stood again for the seat, he turned to his campaign manager, Colonel James Wood, for a plan. In all, some 160 gallons of alcohol were purchased, including a hogshead and a barrel of (strongly spiked) punch, 35 gallons of wine, 43 gallons of strong beer and cider. It was distributed, free of charge—a legal act at the time—to the county's 391 eligible voters. Washington won this time, with 39.04 percent of the vote. In all, it cost him thirty-nine pounds and six shillings. Washington won reelection in 1761.

The Revolutionary War would pull Washington aside, as it would all Americans, from 1765 until 1781. During this time, he took another leadership role, as general, in the fight for independence from Britain. As part of morale for the troops, he saw the allotment of alcohol as an important factor. "There should always be a sufficient quantity of spirits with the army, to furnish moderate supplies to the troops…such as when they are marching in hot or cold weather, in camp in wet, on fatigue or in working parties, it is so essential that it is not to be dispensed with." These were Washington's instructions to the commissary general of purchases for the Continental army in 1777.

After the war ended, Washington returned to his Mount Vernon estate but was called in 1787 to attend the Constitutional Convention in Philadelphia to craft the United States Constitution and address other governing issues. He was elected convention president. At a farewell party with fifty-five folks in attendance, among the following beverages were enjoyed:

- fifty-four bottles of Madeira
- sixty bottles of claret
- eight bottles of Old Stock (a whiskey)
- twenty-two bottles of porter (beer)

- eight bottles of cider
- twelve bottles of beer
- seven large bowls of (boozy) punch

It was noted that the bill included several broken wine decanters, glasses and tumblers. In addition, sixteen servants and musicians downed:

- sixteen bottles of claret
- five bottles Madeira
- seven bowls of punch

The tab was estimated to have been more than $15,000 in present-day dollars.

Two years later, the government we recognize today was formed, and Washington became the nation's first president, being sworn in in New York City. By the time he took office in 1789, he celebrated with others with strong drink as well; one item he insisted on was rum from Barbados, recognized for quality.

Most of the time, the Washingtons ate and drank simply; the president once wrote, "A glass of wine and a bit of mutton are always ready, and such as will be content to partake of them are always welcome." The wine would likely be claret, a bold red vintage. He might also have had on hand a tankard of porter or perhaps a tumbler of Madeira. Sometimes there would be a large gathering, and sometimes the meal was more intimate. On special occasions, he'd break out some rum or a punch. According to those working at George Washington's Mount Vernon, "George Washington held an enlightened, modern attitude toward the consumption of alcohol. He enjoyed a variety of beverages, his favorite being sweet fortified wines like Madeira and Port. He also drank rum punch, porter, and whiskey. He was well aware of the dangers of drinking alcohol to excess and was a strong proponent of moderation."

As president, Washington held more formal affairs each Thursday at 4:00 p.m., with a number of folks invited, most from within the political realm. Fine china would be set, and there could be as many as twenty courses. Senator William Maclay of Pennsylvania described such a meal in his diary entry of August 27, 1789:

> *First was the soup; fish roasted and boiled; meats, gammon* [a smoked or cured ham], *fowls, etc. This was the dinner. The middle of the table was*

garnished in the usual tasty way, with small images, flowers [artificial], *etc. The dessert was, first apple-pies, pudding, etc.; then iced creams, jellies, etc.; then water-melons, musk-melons, apples, peaches, nuts…*

Then the president, filling a glass of wine, with great formality drank to the health of every individual by name round the table. Everybody imitated him, charged glasses, and such a buzz of "health, sir," and "health, madam," and "thank you, sir," and "thank you, madam," never had I heard before…

We did not sit long after the ladies retired. The president rose, went upstairs to drink coffee; the company followed. I took my hat and came home.

Had the dinner been a few years later, the Washingtons might have served the president's own whiskey to end the meal rather than a cup of coffee. After serving two terms as commander in chief, Washington returned home to Mount Vernon in 1797. There, James Anderson, the estate's Scottish farm manager, approached Washington. Anderson had experience with distilling grain both in Scotland and in Virginia, and this experience convinced Washington to build and operate a distillery there. Mount Vernon already had several of the necessary ingredients: grain crops, a water supply and a gristmill.

After initial distilling in a cooperate building, construction on a larger building began in October that year. The stone still house was large enough for five stills, making it one of the largest distilleries in America at that time. While the average distillery measured about 800 square feet, George Washington's distillery was almost three times that size at 2,250 square feet.

The five copper pots got their work out, distilling twelve months a year, a much higher production rate than others at the time. According to George Washington's Mount Vernon, the average Virginia distillery in 1799 produced about 650 gallons of whiskey per year. In the same time frame, Washington's distillery produced almost 11,000 gallons of whiskey.

So, what kind of whiskey did George Washington produce? It was 60 percent rye, 35 percent corn and 5 percent barley. The estate notes that the blend was distilled twice and sold as common whiskey, while smaller amounts were distilled up to four times to make a more premium—and expensive—product. Some were filtered to remove any impurities. Others were flavored with cinnamon or persimmons.

The cost on the common whiskey was about fifty cents per gallon, while the fourth-distilled and filtered (rectified) drink was about one dollar per gallon. Brandy was priced slightly more. When rye was not abundant or not available, wheat was used in its place. Brandies were crafted from apple, peaches and persimmons. Vinegar was also produced.

These products would have gone into thirty-one-gallon barrels; Washington did not bottle any of his spirits. The whiskey would not have been aged; rather, it was shipped to stores, taverns and the like in Alexandria, Richmond and other nearby places. The folks at Mount Vernon note that Washington's closest friend was also his best customer: George Gilpin, who owned a shop in Alexandria.

Some merchants purchased large quantities to resell, while some other farmers traded their grain for the finished product. Folks would also barter products and services. Among the workers at Washington's distillery assisting with whiskey production were six of his slaves: Daniel, Hanson, James, Nat, Peter and Timothy.

Within a decade of the president's death in 1799, the distillery had fallen into disrepair. In 1814, the building itself burned to the ground. Archaeological excavations found the distillery's stone foundation, the location of the copper stills and boiler and other infrastructure. Other items like broken plates, cups and glasses were also uncovered. After research, reconstruction of the building began in 2005. Following the writings of Washington to create a building as close as to the original, the distillery reopened in 2007. The first batch of whiskey, which is distilled in limited quantities and only available for purchase in person, was released to the public in 2010.

In 2017, Governor Terry McAuliffe signed a bill sponsored by Virginia senator Adam Ebbin (D-30th) honoring George Washington's Rye Whiskey as the official spirit of the Commonwealth of Virginia. The whiskey is 60 percent rye, 35 percent corn and 5 percent malted barley.

The Whiskey Rebellion

In order to pay for the large amounts of debt associated with the Revolutionary War, Secretary of the Treasury Alexander Hamilton proposed an excise tax on distilled spirits produced domestically in what would be known as the Whiskey Act. Hamilton argued that it was a luxury tax; he had support with it as a sin tax from others who believed in temperance. It became law in 1791.

There was, however, no support from farmers and others who made whiskey for personal use and who relied on still operation for income. Some argued the hardship of transporting grain to market rather than whiskey. Some said that it would unfairly target folks living in the West.

Although the Whiskey Rebellion is principally rooted in Western Pennsylvania, this isolated, mountainous frontier had opposition across the Appalachia region, including Virginia. Some of the opposition would come in the form of refusal to pay taxes or organized protests. Others turned violent, such as the case of the 1791 whipping, tarring and feathering of tax collector Robert Johnson in Pennsylvania. By the next year, Washington had issued a proclamation that condemned all actions by the westerners that "obstruct the operation of the laws of the United States for raising a revenue upon spirits distilled within the same."

The resistance continued, and escalated, until 1794. An armed group attacked a federal marshal. A tax collector's home was burned. Then, in August that year, Washington called up thirteen thousand men in a militia from Virginia, Maryland, New Jersey and Pennsylvania to meet the resistance with force. He allowed anyone to "disperse and retire peaceably to their respective abodes." Thousands fled into the mountains, fleeing the militia. The leader of the rebellion, David Bradford, escaped the troops, first traveling to New Orleans, then a Spanish territory.

By November, Hamilton was reporting to the president that there were about 150 prisoners. The troops started heading home, and by July 1795, most of those who had been held for the rebellion had either been acquitted for lack of evidence or later pardoned by Washington.

Actions by the administration were viewed popularly, although many folks in the West still made and sold their whiskey without paying tax on it, just more discreetly. In 1802, the distilled spirits excise tax was repealed, at least for a while.

VERY VIRGINIA HOLIDAYS

Christmas is come, hang on the pot,
Let spits turn round, and ovens be hot;
Beef, pork, and poultry, now provide
To feast thy neighbors at this tide;
Then wash all down with good wine and beer,
And so with mirth conclude the Year.
—Virginia Almanac, *1765*

There's a brisk, cold breeze blowing down Duke of Gloucester Street in Colonial Williamsburg, fanning bonfires and scenting the air with burning hardwood. The smoke mixed with the smell of boxwood and pine, which wafted from holiday wreaths and swags decorating doorways and windows.

The sky was dark—a Prussian blue—with moody clouds occasionally giving way to a clear patch revealing tiny, twinkling stars. Indeed, the street was dark, save for the candles in windows of homes and businesses along the thoroughfare and the occasional bonfire.

It was quiet, by and large. Feet shuffled on brick-lined streets. An occasional burst of downy snowflakes fell from the clouds, riding silently on the wind. In the distance, the sound of Christmas carols rang out. Someone stumbled from a tavern.

The scene outside one of the homes was festive, ready for a party. Well-dressed folk mixed together. Songs were sung, tales told and contagious laughter pierced the night. Soon, the doors were thrown open, and the revelers filed in. Immediately, the warmth of the fire thawed cold fingers and toes. Candles flickered on the tables, casting dancing shadows against the wall. A table was set, groaning with Christmas delights of all sorts, from savory to sweet. Another held an enormous punch bowl, filled with the home mistress's special recipe. Another punch bowl on another table held eggnog, with the recipe supposedly from George Washington himself.

This is how many folks imagine eighteenth-century Virginia, and there is some truth as to the fact that Virginians loved a celebration—and still do. As they were able, each class made do the best they could to highlight occurrences from weddings to Christmas. And it didn't have to be in Williamsburg. Festivities played out from the colonial capital to Alexandria and every place in between.

But Christmas was a special time, as noted by Harold B. Gill Jr. in "Christmas in Colonial Virginia" for Colonial Williamsburg in the *Virginia Almanac* in December 1772: "This Month much Meat will be roasted in rich Mens Kitchens, the Cooks sweating in making of minced Pies and other Christmas Cheer, and whole Rivers of Punch, Toddy, Wine, Beer, and Cider consumed with drinking."

In Emma L. Powers's "Christmas Customs" for Colonial Williamsburg, she noted:

> *Wines, brandy, rum punches, and other alcoholic beverages went plentifully around the table on December 25 in well-to-do households.*

Others had less because they could afford less. Slave owners gave out portions of rum and other liquors to their workers at Christmastime, partly as a holiday treat (one the slaves may have come to expect and even demand) and partly to keep slaves at the home quarter during their few days off work. People with a quantity of alcohol in them were more likely to stay close to home than to run away or travel long distances to visit family.

An annual favorite beverage at gatherings was punch. "Punch was a very popular beverage in England and her colonies starting the late seventeenth and early eighteenth centuries. The process of distilling was becoming more refined and widespread in this period, but the tradition of barrel aging sprits had not become common," said Frank Clark, historic foodways supervisor for Colonial Williamsburg.

This means that most spirits at this time were very strong and not suitable for drinking straight. "So, the English borrowed the idea of mixing distilled spirits with water, sugar, spice and citrus juice, from the East Indies and popularized punch," added Clark. He noted that the British also created a cheaper version of punch by leaving out the citrus and spices and just using water, spirits and sugar to create a drink called grog. Some of the more popular punches of the day included Fish House Punch, Hannah Wooley Punch and Regent Punch, although many folks had their own recipe they followed.

One of the beverages enjoyed during this period was wassail, an ancient hot mulled drink, usually crafted from apple cider with alcohol added. It was imbibed to save off winter's chill and to promote health. Indeed, the name comes from the Anglo-Saxon greeting *wass hael*, which means "be whole" or "be well." Typically, in Virginia, the master of the household would pass a bowl of this punch around to others in attendance and repeat the greeting, drinking to their good health.

Wassailers also took to the streets, Nancy Egloff wrote in "Christmas in 17th Century England and Virginia" for the Jamestown Settlement & American Revolution Museum at Yorktown:

Wassailers…paraded to the houses in the towns on Christmas Eve, New Year's Eve and Twelfth Night, traditionally carrying a wassail bowl full of spiced ale, sugar and apples, and singing a wassailing song while passing the bowl:

Wassail! Wassail! All over the town
Our toast it is white, our ale it is brown,
Our bowl it is made of a maplin tree;
We be good fellows all, I drink to thee.

Another holiday favorite was eggnog. "Eggnog is basically a milk punch," said Clark. "The English had a long tradition of mixing alcohol and milk to create a variety of foodstuffs. One of the most popular of these in the eighteenth century was syllabub." He added that another similar concoction was posset. "What sets eggnog apart of these drinks is that in both of those cases the cream was intentionally curdled. With eggnog they replace the curds with whipped egg whites and try not to curdle the cream by adding the alcohol slowly and mixing it in with the egg yolks and sugar before adding the cream."

He continued, "Punch of all types was generally served opposite of the season so in the summer they are chilled, and in the winter, they would be served hot. In fact, there are recipes calling for heated eggnog well into the early twentieth century."

The first cookbook written in America did not contain a mention of eggnog, but just about all the other early ones do, he said. "The southern cookbooks tend to add a peach brandy and use bourbon as the main liquor....One of the most famous recipes for eggnog comes from George Washington. [His] sounds like a pretty potent version of eggnog. It seems that early on this drink becomes associated with the holiday season and is part of the holiday rituals in America by the 1820s."

ANOTHER CENTURY WINDS DOWN

The century began coming to a close, with U.S. government figures showing in 1790 that annual per-capita alcohol consumption for everybody over the age of fifteen amounted to thirty-four gallons of beer and cider, five gallons of distilled spirits and one gallon of wine, noted Colonial Williamsburg.

But why not? "Americans thought alcohol was healthful," according to Ed Crews in his article "Drinking in Colonial America in the Holiday" for the 2007 *Colonial Williamsburg Journal*. "To their minds, drink kept people warm, aided digestion, and increased strength. Not only did alcohol prevent health problems, but it could cure or at least mitigate them. They took whiskey for colic and laryngitis. Hot brandy punch addressed cholera. Rum-soaked cherries helped with a cold. Pregnant women and women in labor received a shot to ease their discomfort."

But as the century came to a close, a push away from alcohol was on the rise. As early as 1800, a temperance movement was formed in Virginia urging the banning of whiskey; other groups popped up in other states. Many subscribed to Benjamin Rush's 1784 piece, "An Inquiry Into the Effects of Ardent Spirits Upon the Human Body and Mind," which eschewed alcoholic beverages and drunkenness.

So prevalent was public intoxication that Benjamin Franklin released "The Drinkers Dictionary" in the *Pennsylvania Gazette* on January 6, 1737, with some two-hundred-plus euphemisms for the word *drunk*. Here's a dozen of our favorites:

- *He is Addled*
- *Bewitch'd*
- *Been at Barbadoes*
- *Cock Ey'd*
- *In his Element*
- *Glaiz'd*
- *Hammerish*
- *Moon-Ey'd*
- *Swampt*
- *Been too free with Sir John Strawberry*
- *Has Swallow'd a Tavern Token*
- *He makes Virginia Fence*

RECIPES

EXCELLENT CHERRY BOUNCE

There were also a lot of funny names for drinks hundreds of years ago: slings, cobblers, rattle-skulls and the bounce.

With a cordial using the freshest fruit available at the time, the alcohol preserves that just-harvested flavor into a sweet, satisfying drink. How satisfying? It was one of George Washington's favorites, and he was even known to carry a canteen full of it on a trip west across the Allegheny Mountains in 1784.

Washington may have done well in naming one of his fifty or so dogs he owned after his beloved cordial; according to the Presidential Pet Museum, he already had hounds named Drunkard, Sweet Lips, Tipler and Tipsy but no Cherry Bounce.

The recipe was found in his wife Martha's papers as "Excellent Cherry Bounce":

Extract the juice of 20 pounds well ripend Morrella cherrys. Add to this 10 quarts of old french brandy and sweeten it with White sugar to your taste. To 5 gallons of this mixture add one ounce of spice such as cinnamon, cloves and nutmegs of each an Equal quantity slightly bruis'd and a pint and half of cherry kirnels that have been gently broken in a mortar. After the liquor has fermented let it stand close-stoped for a month or six weeks then bottle it, remembering to put a lump of Loaf Sugar into each bottle.

Reserve the fruit from the bounce for enjoying with desserts like topping cake or ice cream or adding to sangrias or other drinks. The fruit freezes well for up to six months. Here's how we make ours.

1 pound cherries, stemmed and pitted
2¾ cups sugar
1 cinnamon stick, broken
2 whole cloves
⅛-inch piece fresh nutmeg
4 cups Virginia spirits such as spiced or white rum, bourbon or other whiskey, or vodka

Put the cherries in a bowl, and with a potato masher, mash them thoroughly to release juice. Add the cherries and juice to a 3-quart, sealable glass jar. Add the sugar, cinnamon, cloves, nutmeg and spirits and shake to mix and dissolve the sugar. Place in a sunny, indoor spot, such as next to a window, for one week. Gently shake the bottle and then place it in a cool, dark place indoors, like a cabinet or closet, for forty days.

Transfer contents into a sealable glass quart container through a mesh colander that has been lined with coffee filters or cheesecloth to catch any sediments. Reserve the fruit for desserts or snacking. Yields 12–16 servings.

BOURBON SLUSH

Distilled spirits, especially whiskey, have had a long tradition in Virginia. In 1620, Berkeley Plantation colonist George Thorpe distilled what he said was a "good drinke of Indian corne," akin to moonshine and a precursor to bourbon. Upon retiring as president in 1797, George Washington started a commercial distilling operation—the only Founding Father to do so. The Mount Vernon Ladies' Association has restored the distillery and an adjacent gristmill, located about three miles from the estate.

Virginians have always loved their punch, and this modern one is a crowd pleaser. It puts local spirits to good use and satisfies the southern palate for boozy, sugary drinks with equal parts bourbon, lemonade and sweet ice tea.

4 cups bourbon
4 cups lemonade
4 cups sweet ice tea
1 cup ginger ale

Combine the bourbon, lemonade and tea in a 9x13x2-inch baking dish. Freeze overnight. Remove the frozen mixture from the freezer 30 minutes before serving. Break up the mixture slightly and transfer to a punch bowl. Add the ginger ale. Stir until a slushy consistency is reached and serve immediately. Yields 12–16 cocktails.

GEORGE WASHINGTON'S EGG NOG
(WITH RUM-INFUSED WHIPPED CREAM)

George Washington was America's first president and owner of the country's largest distillery at the time, and apparently he knew how to throw one heck of a party. Case in point: his very boozy eggnog recipe. Rooted in England, eggnog was a signature holiday drink in Colonial America. Bottoms up, fellow patriots:

Take a quart cream, one quart milk, one dozen tablespoons sugar, one pint brandy, pint rye whiskey, pint Jamaica rum, pint sherry—mix liquor first, then separate yolks and whites of 12 eggs, add sugar to beaten yolks, mix well. Add milk and cream, slowly beating. Beat whites of eggs until stiff and fold slowly into mixture. Let set in cool place for several days. Taste frequently.

When it comes time to spike your eggnog, the author humbly suggests Four Farthing Spiced Rum, a historically inspired offering that the author created in partnership with Virginia Beach–based Chesapeake Bay Distillery; it's a richly flavored, refined rum based on spices that would have been found in ships calling port in the region in the seventeenth and eighteenth centuries. Here's our version.

Eggnog
2 whole eggs, plus 1 egg yolk
½ cup sugar
½ teaspoon cinnamon
½ teaspoon nutmeg
2½ cups milk
½ cup heavy cream
Virginia spirits, such as spiced or white rum, bourbon or other whiskey or moonshine
rum-infused whipping cream

Rum-Infused Whipping Cream
1 cup heavy whipping cream
⅓ cup confectioners' sugar
2 teaspoons spiced or white rum (you may also use another Virginia spirit such as bourbon or other whiskey, or moonshine)

To make the eggnog, in a medium bowl add whole eggs and egg yolk, sugar, cinnamon and nutmeg and whisk to incorporate. In a medium saucepan over medium heat, add milk and heavy cream, stir and heat to just under a boil. Remove from heat and temper the eggs by adding a little hot milk into the bowl at a time, whisking and stirring continually; pour the mixture back into the saucepan and heat on low, stirring until thick, about 3–5 minutes. Do not boil. Strain into a bowl, cool to room temperature, cover and refrigerate.

To make the whipped cream, chill a medium metal bowl and a metal whisk a few hours beforehand. In the bowl, pour the heavy whipping cream along with the sugar and spirit. Whisk vigorously until soft peaks form, about 5 minutes. Cover and refrigerate until ready for use (use soon).

To assemble the drink, before serving, stir in a half cup of Virginia spirits such as bourbon or other whiskey, moonshine or rum. Transfer to mugs and serve each topped with prepared rum-infused whipped cream and a sprinkling of cinnamon and nutmeg.
Yields 4–6 servings.

FISH HOUSE PUNCH

Virginians, indeed all colonial Americans, drank a lot of punch, according to Colonial Williamsburg's Frank Clark. Perhaps one of the most enduring punches of the time was Fish House Punch, a boozy rum concoction with peach brandy and other intoxicating ingredients, served in a large punch bowl with a large ice block in the center and with many lemon slices garnishing the drink.

The punch was first created in 1732 at The State in Schuylkill, colloquially known as the Fish House, a Philadelphia fishing club. It was a Virginian who first noted the drink in 1744 when a diplomat, who was visiting the club, wrote that it was "a Bowl of fine Lemon Punch big enough to have Swimmed half a dozen of young Geese."

Its strength was noted in a poem of the time:

> *There's a little place just out of town,*
> *Where, if you go to lunch,*
> *They'll make you forget your mother-in-law*
> *With a drink called Fish-House Punch.*

For the longest time, the recipe was secret and even changed occasionally—the original is anyone's guess. Although variations (often called Fish House Punch) were served far and wide—including taverns across the Old Dominion—when the punch was prepared at the club, it was done so with much pomp and circumstance, with participating members wearing "white aprons and straw boaters," according to Janet Clarkson in *Food History Almanac*. She noted, "Since 1812 it has been mixed in an especially commissioned nine-gallon Chinese porcelain bowl emblazoned with the club emblem of a perch."

This recipe is based on the 1873 instructions of club governor Dr. William Camac, with some touches added in keeping with the history of the drink:

> 1 ¼ pounds confectioners' sugar
> 4 ½ cups water
> 1 cup fresh lemon juice
> 1 cup cognac
> 1 cup white rum
> ½ cup peach brandy or peach schnapps
> lemon slices

In a large bowl, add the sugar with two cups of water and stir until dissolved. Add the lemon juice to the sugar water. Add the remaining water, cognac, rum and peach brandy or peach schnapps. Serve in glasses over crushed ice and with a lemon slice garnish.
Yields 6–8 cocktails.

HAUTE CHOCOLATE

Chocolate was first mentioned in the New World as early as 1641 and in North America by 1705. According to Colonial Williamsburg, by 1773, the colonies were importing more than 320 tons of cocoa beans. "Drinking chocolate was affordable to all classes of people and was available in most coffee houses, where colonists would gather to talk about politics and the news of the day," said Rodney Snyder of Mars Chocolate for Colonial Williamsburg.

Chocolate came in block form, which was easy to transport and keep; it was used as a ration for soldiers during the American Revolution. It would remain enjoyed in drinking form until the mid-nineteenth century. Chocolate was served as a drink in Colonial Virginia and throughout the other American colonies in the eighteenth century, commonly at public coffeehouses alongside coffee and tea. The environment offered a more subdued place to sit and meet others for drinks and discourse outside of a tavern. Chocolate was also served in private homes, and sometimes wine or a spirit might be added to make it a boozy treat.

"The most common was chocolate wine, making drinking chocolate but instead of using water or milk they would use a port or Madeira. Other than that, not a lot of mentions of adding spirits to chocolate; if they did it was probably brandy or perhaps a rum," said Frank Clark of Colonial Williamsburg.

So, we offer two versions of hot chocolate that are inspired by our ancestors' penchant for cocoa.

Wine Hot Chocolate
1 pint red wine
4 ounces unsweetened chocolate, chopped
1 tablespoon sugar
½ teaspoon ground cinnamon
¼ teaspoon cayenne pepper

Heat wine in a saucepan over medium heat to just below the simmering point. Remove the pan from the heat and add the chocolate. When chocolate has melted, add the sugar, cinnamon and cayenne and whisk to combine. Pour into two mugs while still hot and top with Rum-Infused Whipped Cream (see recipe earlier). Yields 2 cups.

Spiked Hot Chocolate
1 pint milk
4 ounces unsweetened chocolate, chopped
1 tablespoon sugar
½ teaspoon ground cinnamon
¼ teaspoon ground nutmeg
4 ounces Virginia spirits such as spiced or white rum, or whiskey such as bourbon or rye

Heat milk in a saucepan over medium heat to just below the simmering point. Remove the pan from the heat and add the chocolate. When chocolate has melted, add the sugar, cinnamon and nutmeg and whisk to combine. Pour 2 ounces of Virginia spirits

into two mugs and top off with hot chocolate while still hot. Garnish with Rum-Infused Whipped Cream (see recipe earlier).
Yields 2 cups.

RYE AND GINGER

This is a simple, modern drink made to enjoy one of Virginia's historic whiskeys: rye. It became natural for farmers to produce what grew well in their soil as they moved away from Coastal Virginia and headed west; corn and rye were two of those grains. And as those farmers and others in the area began making distilled spirits, it was corn and rye that became the mash that turned into whiskey. The popularity increased as it became a larger part of the market and as Americans eschewed rum due to anti-British sentiment leading up to and during the American Revolutionary War.

"As early as the 1730s, records have been found of Virginia farmers growing rye and distilling their own whiskey for pleasure and trade. Now those traditions are being born again. A new generation of Virginia distillers are sourcing heritage rye grains from family farms across the commonwealth and making a little history of their own," noted the folks at Virginia Rye Whiskey, a group of Old Dominion distillers promoting the product and its heritage.

Rye has a distinct, complex flavor with characteristic liveliness and goes well with the forwardness of the ginger and the citrus pop in this drink. For a milder ginger flavor, you could substitute ginger ale in place of the ginger beer.

4 ounces ginger beer
2 ounces rye whiskey
1 tablespoon fresh lime juice
lime slice

Add ice about halfway in a glass. Pour in the ginger beer, rye and lime juice and stir to blend. Top with ice and garnish with a lime slice.
Yields 1 cocktail.

SANGAREE

Like so many imbibes in the eighteenth century, sangaree is a type of punch and was a popular eighteenth-century drink. It was first noted in *British Gentleman's Magazine* in a 1736 issue as "a punch seller in the Strand had devised a new punch made of strong Madeira wine and called Sangre." It seems, however, that the drink may have actually had its origin in the Antilles and possibly other Caribbean islands. It became a favorite drink throughout American colonies.

The beverage's name comes from the Spanish word *sangre*, meaning blood, for its blood-red hue. It's a precursor to the more commonly known sangria, which was also enjoyed in Colonial Virginia.

Sangaree was traditionally made with a fortified wine, such as Madeira or even port; we use a favorite red wine of ours that we have on hand, preferably a Virginia wine. We further enhance the drink with a spirit like gin or rum; we like gin with this drink as a nod to the London Gin Craze of the era.

1 lemon wedge
¼ ounce simple syrup or ½ teaspoon confectioners' sugar
1½ ounces red wine
1 ounce gin or rum
1 lemon slice
fresh nutmeg

In a cocktail shaker, squeeze lemon wedge and toss in. Add syrup/sugar, wine, gin/rum and ice. Shake and strain in coupe glass. Garnish with a lemon slice and a dusting of nutmeg. Yields 1 cocktail.

SANGAREE ICE

Use prepared sangaree to create ice cubes to add to cocktails throughout the holiday season. As the cubes melt, they add flavor and color to the

Sangaree cocktail at Still Worldly Eclectic Tapas in Portsmouth. The vintage Colonial Williamsburg capitol building replica decanter is part of the author's culinary collection. *Cocktail by Karl Dornemann, photo by Lucas Pomianek; author's collection.*

drink you are enjoying. We especially enjoy adding a cube or two to a flute of champagne.

double batch of sangaree, prepared

Pour prepared sangaree into ice cube trays, add a thin slice of lemon and freeze. Once frozen, remove and store in ziptop bags in freezer. Remove cubes as needed and add to beverages.

MULLED WINE

Like wassail, mulled wine has been enjoyed since time immemorial to warm bones during the chilly times of the year. It's not just the heat of the warm wine itself that creates a sense of well-being, but the earthy spices added as well. Of course, the shot of whiskey doesn't hurt either.

Mulled wine was thought to have begun with the Greeks and spread by the Romans. As the Romans conquered parts of Europe, the tradition grew as well. By the Middle Ages, mulled wine was being consumed to not only take off a chill but for perceived medicinal purposes as well. It was a tradition brought from England to Virginia and all of Colonial America.

In the next century, a version of mulled wine, called the Smoking Bishop, would be immortalized in Charles Dickens's novel *A Christmas Carol*.

2 quarts red wine
1 ½ cups freshly-squeezed orange juice
1 tablespoon dark brown sugar
2–3 cinnamon sticks
1 teaspoon ground cinnamon
1 teaspoon ground cloves
1 teaspoon ground ginger
juice of one lemon
12 ounces whiskey
cinnamon sticks
orange peel
star anise

In a Dutch oven over medium-high heat, add wine, orange juice, brown sugar, cinnamon sticks, ground cinnamon, ground cloves, ground ginger and lemon juice and bring to a boil. Reduce the heat and simmer for 2 hours. Serve hot in mugs, adding 1½ ounces of whiskey to each serving and garnish with a cinnamon stick, orange peel and one whole star anise. Yields 8 servings.

WASSAIL

Wassail was just one of the hot, mulled drinks enjoyed during cold months in Virginia, across the American colonies and back in England during the eighteenth century. An ancient drink going back hundreds of years, it had a base of apple cider heated and complementary citrus flavors that added punch. Earthy spices like cinnamon, cloves and ginger gave warmth beyond the heated mug.

But it wasn't just a drink—it was also an activity. It became a tradition for folks to go from house to house during the holiday period wassailing, or caroling, as in this nineteenth-century folk song:

> *Here we come a-wassailing*
> *Among the leaves so green;*
> *Here we come a-wand'ring*
> *So fair to be seen.*
> *Love and joy come to you,*
> *And to you your wassail too;*
> *And God bless you and send you a Happy New Year*
> *And God send you a Happy New Year.*

Once finished singing, the wassailers would enjoy a hot mug of the punch and perhaps line their wallets with a half-penny or two from the hosts.

A number of spirits could be used to enhance the wassail; in our version, we, like a number of Virginia distillates, include spiced rum, bourbon, moonshine or vodka.

2 quarts apple cider
1½ cups freshly squeezed orange juice

½ cup freshly squeezed lemon juice
3–4 cinnamon sticks, broken
2–3 tablespoons brown sugar
1 teaspoon ground cinnamon
½ teaspoon ground cloves
½ teaspoon ground ginger
1–2 cups Virginia spirits such as spiced or white rum, bourbon or other whiskey,
moonshine, or vodka
cinnamon sticks
orange peel
star anise

In a large Dutch oven over medium-high heat, add the cider, orange and lemon juices, cinnamon sticks, brown sugar, ground cinnamon, ground cloves and ground ginger; do not boil. Reduce heat and simmer, covered, for 2 hours. Remove from heat, add spirits and serve in mugs garnished with a cinnamon stick, orange peel and whole star anise. Yields 8–10 servings.

HOT BUTTERED RUM

Hot toddies are simply alcoholic beverages that were served warm, such as hot buttered rum. A recipe in 1786 defined it as a "beverage made of alcoholic liquor with hot water, sugar, and spices." A predecessor of hot buttered rum was documented as early as 1594, when Thomas Dawson described "Buttered Beere," which included beer, eggs, sugar, nutmeg, clove, ginger and sweet butter bubbling away over a fire in a pewter pot.

As the New World was explored, and as rum became the fashionable drink of the seventeenth and much of the eighteenth centuries, a similar concoction was crafted using that distilled spirit instead. Here is our version.

1 tablespoon room-temperature butter
1 teaspoon dark brown sugar
1 teaspoon good vanilla extract
½ teaspoon ground cinnamon
½ teaspoon ground nutmeg

2 ounces rum
8 ounces hot water
cinnamon stick

Place the butter, brown sugar, vanilla, cinnamon and nutmeg in the bottom of a tall coffee mug and muddle with an iced tea spoon. Add rum and hot water and stir; serve immediately. Garnish with a cinnamon stick. Yields 1 cocktail.

Chapter 3

THE NINETEENTH CENTURY

CHEERS, FOR SOME, TO A NEW CENTURY

America was a brand-spanking-new nation, and many changes were in store at the cusp of a new century. The country still loved its alcohol, and people pretty much drank it from morning until night. But at this point, many folks imbibing had shifted from small beer and lower-alcohol ciders consumed in the seventeenth and eighteenth centuries to downing hard liquor—and lots of it. According to the 1810 census, there were more than 14,000 distilleries in the young nation, with more than 3,600 in Virginia, to keep up with the demand.

And remember that federal excise tax that was placed on liquor that caused the Whiskey Rebellion in the late 1700s? On the recommendation of Virginia-born Thomas Jefferson, who became the third president in 1801 (after John Adams), it was abolished the year he took office.

By 1830, American adults were drinking seven gallons of pure alcohol per capita annually, according to Daniel Orkent in his book *Last Call: The Rise and Fall of Prohibition*. Today, according to the World Health Organization, adults in the United States are drinking about three and a half gallons per capita annually of alcohol in 2016—a significant difference.

In 1839, Frederick Marryat, an English traveler, noted this in his book *A Diary in America* about the nation's love affair with booze: "I am sure the Americans can fix nothing without a drink. If you meet, you drink; if you part, you drink; if you make acquaintance, you drink; if you close a bargain you drink; they quarrel in their drink, and they make it up with a drink.

They drink because it is hot; they drink because it is cold. If successful in elections, they drink and rejoice; if not, they drink and swear; they begin to drink early in the morning, they leave off late at night; they commence it early in life, and they continue it, until they soon drop into the grave."

Alcohol consumption would drop off a bit, but not before having a heyday by century's end in the Gay Nineties. But not everyone shared the excitement in raising a glass, or two, or three. The seeds of temperance were being sown, and they would grab root and begin to flourish throughout the 1800s before finally taking hold as Prohibition slightly more than one hundred years later.

Although the concepts of temperance and prohibition were suggested—even briefly made into law—in the colonies off and on since the seventeenth century, it was the writings of one of the signers of the Declaration of Independence that struck a nerve. In 1784, Founding Father Benjamin Rush spoke of the evils of alcohol in his paper "An Inquiry Into the Effects of Ardent Spirits Upon the Human Body and Mind." An addendum in 1790 was called "A Moral and Physical Thermometer." In it, water and small (low alcohol) beer provided "serenity of mind, reputation, long life, & happiness." If you drank cider or perry, wine, porter or strong beer, you could be assured of "cheerfulness, strength, and nourishment, when taken only in small quantities, and at meals." But punch, toddy and egg rum, grog, shrubs, bitter-infused spirits and cordials, drams of gin, brandy and rum in the morning, day or night led to vices including idleness and murder, diseases from puking to madness and punishments from the poorhouse to the gallows.

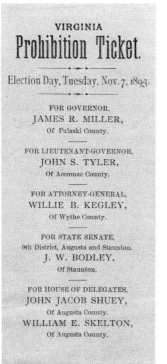

VIRGINIA
Prohibition Ticket.

Election Day, Tuesday, Nov. 7, 1893.

FOR GOVERNOR,
JAMES R. MILLER,
Of Pulaski County.

FOR LIEUTENANT-GOVERNOR,
JOHN S. TYLER,
Of Accomac County.

FOR ATTORNEY-GENERAL,
WILLIE B. KEGLEY,
Of Wythe County.

FOR STATE SENATE,
9th District, Augusta and Staunton.
J. W. BODLEY,
Of Staunton.

FOR HOUSE OF DELEGATES,
JOHN JACOB SHUEY,
Of Augusta County.
WILLIAM E. SKELTON,
Of Augusta County.

The move to make Virginia, as well as the nation, dry was an important mission to many. Stacking political positions was paramount, as seen in this November 7, 1893 listing of candidates sympathetic to the cause. *Author's collection.*

It was enough to get some folks to sit up and take notice. As early as 1800, a temperance movement was being formed in Virginia urging the banning of whiskey; other groups popped up in other states. Before the middle of the century, groups supporting making alcohol illegal were popping up across the state and the country, and their activities were documented in local newspapers.

One piece singing the virtues of temperance in the *Alexandria Phenix Gazette* of May 21, 1830, also gave a warning to the readers who partook of alcoholic beverages: "Intemperance sears the conscience—it breaks down the barriers between virtue and vice; and oversteps the dividing line of right and wrong—from this cause along 8-10th of your criminals are arraigned at the bars of your courts—some of whom are destined to pine away a solitary existence in the gloomy cells of a penitentiary."

A temperance society in Middleburg reported on a recent meeting in the October 11, 1836 *Alexandria Gazette* that it changed "their character of voluntary benevolence, into declamatory morality and denunciatory religion, by arrogantly declaring 'the temperate use of any and every alcoholic drink, and also the use of wine at the Sacrament, to be immoral and sinful.'"

Already here—less than a half century after Benjamin Rush's work on temperance and allowing for moderation of certain lesser alcoholic beverages like small beer, or cider wine and the like with a meal—folks were adopting a zero-tolerance policy.

The State Temperance Convention, held in Charlottesville in August 1853, was the subject of an article from the State Central Committee that ran in the *Staunton Spectator* on June 1, 1853. It's obvious that complete prohibition of alcohol was also on the minds of those involved, as it read, "The object of this Convention will be to promote the Temperance reformation generally, and especially to consider the great question—what shall be done to secure

Detail of "Uncle Sam's 'Crazes' Past and Present," by Frederick Burr Opper, July 29, 1896. The political cartoon includes the rise of the temperance crusade of the era. *Library of Congress.*

the prohibition of the Liquor Traffic in Virginia,—and to devise the means of prosecuting, vigorously, this reform, until the work is accomplished."

Some of these early temperance movements lost their steam with the Civil War, as the nation's attention turned to other matters at hand, but in the second half of the nineteenth century, groups like the Woman's Christian Temperance Union (WCTU) formed and gained traction.

Raise the Bar and the Restaurant and the Hotel

By the nineteenth century, taverns—sometimes called ordinaries—had been part of the Virginia landscape for going on two hundred years. They had done the Commonwealth well in providing many amenities, from being rest stops and meeting houses to providing overnight lodging and, of course, by being places to get something to eat and drink.

While the colony was growing, these stops connected rural areas, spaced apart to provide a place of rest and refueling for weary travelers and their horses. In towns, they were meeting places and provided a space to exchange news and ideas. There was no consistency with the quality of taverns, however. Some were large and well-run inns, with excellent lodgings and food. Others were tiny and tidy but had little else to write home about. Some were disorganized with bad service, bad food and bad drink.

It seems that many folks just accepted taverns as part of the everyday fabric of life. Then, in the 1800s, that started to change. "From colonial times to the mid-19th century you had taverns, which provided food and lodging," said Christine Sismondo, author of *America Walks into a Bar* in an interview for *Smithsonian Magazine*. "They had a tapster in a cage—as opposed to at a long bar—and it was open to all members of the community, including women and children. Then you start to see the dedicated saloon, which didn't necessarily serve food, and mixed cordials and spirits at a long bar. Women were rarely allowed. Hotel bars existed on the high end, catering to business travelers."

Of note on word usage: words like *inn* and *ordinary* were often used interchangeably for the word *tavern*; there were also several words that were used to describe a place to grab a drink in a hotel or restaurant. Although sometimes this included *club* or *pub*, it increasingly became *bar* or *saloon*.

Figuring out the etymology of the word *bar* is pretty simple. As the design of drinking establishments shifted to include a long barrier, or bar, between the patrons and persons serving the drink, the name as a whole

The "Commercial Drummer's Thanksgiving—The Last Good Story—Scene in an Old Virginia Tavern" from *Frank Leslie's Illustrated Newspaper*, November 1885. Before the turn of the twentieth century, "drummer" meant traveling salesperson, because they "drummed up business." Here the drummers are enjoying some holiday cheer. *Author's collection.*

stuck. Folks no longer ordered their drinks and walked them back to tables; they sat at the bar on stools and engaged the person making the drink, or the bartender.

Another word with popular usage coming about at this time was *saloon*, which is an Anglicized version of the French word *salon*. Saloons in the East were very different from saloons in the western frontier; they were often larger than bars and more often found in hotels. But by and large, nineteenth-century Virginians used the words *bar* and *saloon* interchangeably.

The word usage shift is well exhibited throughout Virginia newspapers and other public notices with the use of the word *bar* in publications. Restaurateur J. Boulanger announced in the January 12, 1837 *Alexandria Gazette* the opening of a new American and French restaurant "nearly opposite Gadsby's" that, in addition to his larder, always supplied "with the delicacies of the season" and cooking "of the most superior description" that "his bar is supplied with choice Wines, Spirits, and Liqueurs." This is a very early use of the word *bar* in Virginia publications. The Gadsby's referenced in the advertisement was Gadsby's Tavern and City Hotel.

There was also well-documented use of the word *saloon*, such as this advertisement in the November 28, 1845 issue of the *Richmond Enquirer*:

> *Our House. The proprietor of the above favorite Restaurant returns his tanks to his friends and patrons, for past favors, and respectfully gives notice, that he has fitted up a Saloon in a style of elegance superior to any other establishment in this city, for the accommodation of his guests; where they can be supplied with all the good things that our own and the Northern Markets afford, at short notice.*
>
> *Orders for oysters opened, in the shell, or game of all kinds, promptly attended to and sent to all parts of the State. C.G. THOMPSON.*

Most interestingly, all of this was coming about as taverns were on the way out, replaced not only by bars and saloons but also by hotels and restaurants, many of which often had their own bars and saloons. Interesting, too, is that this was occurring in a rather small time frame. It's all part and parcel of ushering in the way we drink (and eat) today.

Consider the restaurant. The tavern did not offer a typical restaurant experience—although it served eats and drinks, it offered a *prix fixe* offering at a preset time, not a menu of options at a time of one's choosing. That changed with the French Revolution in the latter part of the eighteenth century. The democratization and cultural shift in France relaxed many rules, including monopolies on food service. Opportunities emerged not just for cooks—who were looking for gainful employment after the dissolution of aristocratic houses—but for middle-class diners too. A new market of food service, with meals prepared by anyone with the desire and skills to prepare them, was open to a new market of customers. From this came a *carte*, or "menu."

A diner could sit down, make a selection from any number of offerings and have it prepared to order. Diners would pay the same prices for the same portion sizes. Food would be presented to diners on individual plates rather than a communal platter or pot being passed around. The basis of the word *restaurant* comes from the French words for *restore* and *restoratives*, given that the enriching bouillons, broths, consommés and soups often served were meant to restore one's strength.

The concept spread from France to Boston in 1794; according to David S. Shields, a noted food historian and the Carolina Distinguished Professor at the University of South Carolina, it had spread to Virginia by the early eighteenth century. In Virginia, the first true restaurant was Daniel Schelling's Restorative, according to Shields. Schelling advertised the opening of his

A "rather seedy" patron at a Virginia tavern, as sketched by noted nineteenth-century artist and storyteller Porte Crayon in his 1857 book *Virginia Illustrated*. Author's collection.

RATHER SEEDY.

restaurant in the September 4, 1820 edition of the *Norfolk American Beacon*. It was located in "the fire proof house belonging to Mr. Arthur Taylor, the third door above the Post Office."

The restaurant offered "superior coffee, early in the morning," as well as soup prepared "every day, by eleven o'clock" in the morning and "beef steaks, oysters, or other relishes" at any time until ten o'clock in the evening. No other information about Schelling has been found, according to Shields. "Whatever the case, he should be recognized as the first restaurateur in the Old Dominion," he noted.

Like restaurants, hotels modernized aspects of taverns too. "Prior to 1820, taverns dominated as drinking establishments, but their replacement by hotels with their 'hotel bars' offered an alternative, and by 1850 saloons were prominent," according to the exhibition "Indomitable Spirits: Prohibition in the United States" on the Digital Public Library of America website.

Taverns also provided a vastly inconsistent product, as noted by George Washington. From 1789 to 1791, Washington took time to formally visit all original thirteen colonies, starting with New England and cumulating with the Southern Tour. In his detailed diary, he described the people, places and things he encounters, including many of the taverns he stayed at during his time on thousands of miles of dusty, rutted roads. Some of the taverns passed muster and some didn't. From his diary:

> OCTOBER 15, 1789
> *"We proceed'd to the Tavern of a Mrs. Haviland at Rye; who keeps a very neat and decent Inn."*

> OCTOBER 21, 1789
> *"Mr. Lyman, and many other Gentlemen sat an hour or two with me in the evening at Parson's Tavern, where I lodged, and which is a good House."*

> NOVEMBER 8, 1789
> *"I stayed at Perkins' tavern (which, by the bye, is not a good one,) all day."*

As A.K. Sandoval-Strausz wrote in "How America Invented the Hotel: A History of Hospitality" in *Slate* magazine: "American inns and taverns were kept in small, unimpressive buildings, mostly dwelling houses that were indistinguishable from homes but for the signs hanging outside. Inside, patrons squeezed into bars that were little more than living rooms with built-in wooden cages where the liquor was kept.…Overnight guests had to put up with a more intimate form of crowding—they were expected to share not just their rooms, but their beds as well."

He added that the first hotels in the United States were built in the 1790s: "These 19th century hotels were recognizably modern not just because of their physical structure but also their social character. American hotels were famously gregarious places. Because hotelkeepers still couldn't turn a profit on room charges alone, they needed to attract local people into their premises and sell them food and especially drinks. Hoteliers offered comfortable and elegant interiors, and townspeople happily congregated in hotel parlors, dining halls, barrooms, and lobbies."

That was the case with the Old Market Hotel in Richmond, as noted in the April 22, 1845 *Richmond Enquirer*. There George E. Sadler said of the hotel, "The Table of the Hotel is always supplied with the best the market affords, and all the seasonable luxuries prepared in the most choice manner—[the] cuisine is faultless, and the most fastidious epicurean can be suited." He continued, "The Bar is stocked with the most choice Wines and Liquors. This department of the Hotel, also, will be found faultless."

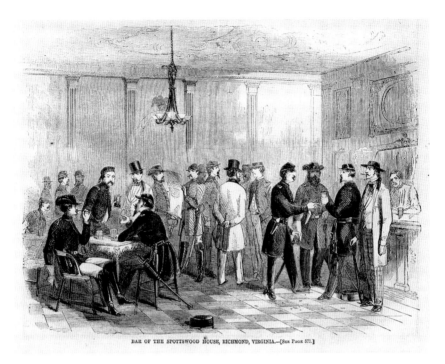

BAR OF THE SPOTTSWOOD HOUSE, RICHMOND, VIRGINIA.—[See Page 571.]

"Bar of the Spottswood House, Richmond," engraving from *Harper's Weekly*, September 1861, showing imbibes being enjoyed. *Author's collection.*

Throughout the late eighteenth and into the early twentieth centuries, Virginia built many grand hotels, not only offering luxurious overnight lodging but also spacious lobbies with bars and saloons for discriminating imbibers. Among them included the following.

GADSBY'S TAVERN

Gadsby's Tavern, Alexandria, was built around 1785, and the adjacent City Hotel was built in 1792. Early on, both were centers of business, political and social life. George Washington was a frequent guest, and other patrons included John Adams, Thomas Jefferson, James Madison, James Monroe and the Marquis de Lafayette. Over time, the property fell in disrepair and saw other uses until its restoration. Today, it is operated as a museum and restaurant. The museum is a stop on the American Whiskey Trail. OPEN.

HYGEIA HOTEL

Hygeia Hotel, Old Point Comfort/Hampton, was a luxurious inn for visitors. It was first opened in 1821 to take in the sea breezes from the Chesapeake

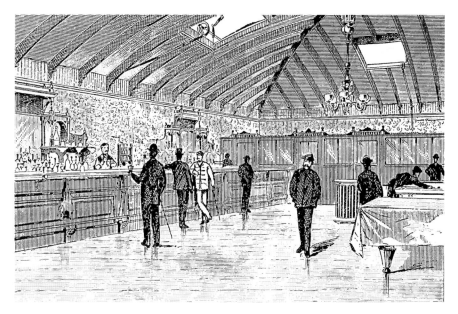

The Hygeia, the bar and the billiard room, circa 1880, Hampton. *Author's collection.*

Bay. It was razed in 1863 during the Civil War, but a restaurant was opened in its place. In 1868, a second Hygeia Hotel was built and elevated to one of the most prominent resorts in the nation. It was demolished in 1902. A large bar and billiards room was promoted in a circa 1880 promotional book. CLOSED.

The Martha Washington Inn
The Martha Washington Inn, Abingdon, is an upscale lodge built in 1832 originally as a residence; it served many functions, among them a women's college, a Civil War hospital and barracks and a residence for visiting actors of the Barter Theatre before becoming an inn in 1935. Many famous guests have stayed there, including Elizabeth Taylor, First Ladies Eleanor Roosevelt and Lady Bird Johnson and Presidents Harry Truman and Jimmy Carter. The inn is noted for its numerous ghosts. Sisters, An American Grill, offers an upscale bar area. OPEN.

The Jefferson
The Jefferson, Richmond, is a palatial hotel in the Spanish Baroque style built in 1895. It has hosted many famous guests, including Charles Lindbergh, Elvis Presley and the Rolling Stones. The hotel was once noted for alligators

living in the lobby pools (now replaced with bronze statues). There are several dining options, and at Lemaire—named after Thomas Jefferson's maître d'hotel, Etienne Lemaire—the marbled-walled, chandeliered bar is simply stunning, whether one is having a casual bite and drink or just enjoying an imbibe. OPEN.

THE CHAMBERLAIN

The Chamberlain, Old Point Comfort/Hampton, is an opulent resort that was first opened in 1896 next door to the Hygeia Hotel. By the end of the twentieth century, the building had become worn, and the appeal as a seaside resort was waning. Major renovations were undertaken, and in 2008, it was reopened as a luxury retirement community. Despite that, the dining room of the Chamberlin is open to the public for certain meals, affording delightful cuisine and sweeping views of the Chesapeake Bay. OPEN.

THE MONTICELLO HOTEL

The Monticello Hotel, Norfolk, is a lavish hotel taking up an entire city block; it was first built in 1898. Following a 1918 fire, it reopened on the same spot in 1919. It was torn down in 1976. The facility housed several cafés and restaurants, including the grandly appointed mahogany bar that the late historian George Tucker recalled in a visit with his father in 1915:

> *The place was such a splendid combination of marble columns, beveled mirrors, potted palms and gilt-framed oil painting of voluptuous nudes it never occurred to me to question why my father's drinks were served in a small shot glass while my ginger ale came in a bottle. But childhood is not an age of speculation, and even though my nose told me my father's libation was different than mine, I brushed that detail aside and concentrated on the luscious painted damsels instead.*

CLOSED.

STONEWALL JACKSON HOTEL

Stonewall Jackson Hotel, Staunton, was built in 1924 as a well-appointed hotel in the Colonial Revival style. In addition to other dining options, there is Sorrel's Lounge, named after the Civil War general's horse, which offers casual bites and cocktails. OPEN.

THE GEORGE WASHINGTON HOTEL

The George Washington Hotel, Winchester, built in 1924, is a luxury property noted for its long association with the Shenandoah Apple Blossom Festival. In addition to other dining options, the charming lobby bar, Half Note Lounge, is noted for live entertainment and is a great place to grab a drink and people watch. OPEN.

THE CAVALIER HOTEL

The Cavalier Hotel, Virginia Beach, built in 1927, is a grande dame overlooking the Atlantic Ocean. Among the visitors were F. Scott Fitzgerald and his wife, Zelda; Judy Garland; Will Rogers; Herbert Hoover; Harry S Truman; John F. Kennedy; Richard Nixon; and Pharrell Williams. The Cavalier began to fall into disrepair. In 2013, developer Bruce Thompson purchased the hotel for $35.1 million to create a five-star resort. After three

Hotels were noted for their opulent bars, such as the Sir Walter Raleigh Lounge inside The Cavalier in Virginia Beach, circa 1933. Note the colonial influence. *Author's collection.*

years and more than $80 million in renovations, the Cavalier reopened in 2018. It features several dining rooms, the Raleigh Room, a bar and the Tarnished Truth Distillery, producing craft spirits. OPEN.

THE MIMSLYN INN

The Mimslyn Inn, Luray, is a classic southern mansion-style hotel built in 1931. In addition to restaurant options, there is also the Speakeasy bar, where one can grab a cocktail. OPEN.

THE WILLIAMSBURG INN

The Williamsburg Inn, Williamsburg, is an eighteenth century–inspired luxury hotel built in 1937 in Colonial Williamsburg still open today. On site is the Rockefeller Room and other dining options, as well as the Social Terrace, a patio extension to the inn's main lobby with an outdoor bar overlooking the Golden Horseshoe Golf Club. Why does Golden Horseshoe sound familiar? It's the name of the Alexander Spotswood 1716 exploration across the Blue Ridge Mountains. OPEN.

ICE, ICE BABY, YEAR-ROUND

In the 1913 book *Ye Ancient History of Norfolk in Ragtime* by Frank S. Wing, the author recalled:

> *Officially, the coldest day on record locally was January 23, 1857, when the thermometer registered five degrees below zero at 7 a.m. The Elizabeth was frozen solidly enough to permit the crossing of pedestrians and vehicles for several days and a barroom was built in the center of the river, being the first time on record when hot Tom and Jerries were served on ice.*
>
> *The saloon did a rushing business, and a number of Norfolk and Portsmouth people are said to have slipped out there after a few drinks.*

There once was a time that if you wanted ice in your drink, it was no problem—as long as it was wintertime, such as the case of the frozen Elizabeth River between the Coastal Virginia towns of Norfolk and Portsmouth. But in most southern states, ice was an elusive commodity for much of the year. Farther north, ice, harvested in blocks during the winter from frozen ponds, could be stashed away insulated in grass, sawdust and straw at icehouses and pits and used year-round, whether for icing down drinks or keeping foods cold.

"Ye Ancient History of Norfolk in Ragtime," illustration from 1913, showing the barroom built on the solidly frozen Elizabeth River, midway between Norfolk and Portsmouth, when temperatures dipped to five below zero in January 1857. *Author's collection.*

Ice was seen as important to Virginians from the beginning. In 1637, Virginia governor Sir William Berkeley was granted a patent by King Charles to sell ice in the colony. George Washington got a taste for ice when living in the Philadelphia home of Robert Morris, used as the presidential mansion at the time. Morris had an ice pit, and Washington enjoyed his drinks cooled.

When he returned to Mount Vernon, he tried to construct a similar icehouse there, but the climate and materials did not work. He wrote to Morris in 1784 that by June, "not the smallest particle" of ice remained. Later improvements allowed Washington to keep ice until August but not year-round. Jefferson also constructed an icehouse at his Monticello estate outside Charlottesville in 1802, constructed in a sixteen-foot-deep pit. It often allowed him to keep ice until September or October.

For folks who did not have icehouses, the frozen water trade between North and South began around the turn of the nineteenth century, led by

Ice was shipped south, including to Virginia, from lakes and ponds in the Northeast during the eighteenth century, as shown in this circa 1900 postcard of ice harvesting at Wenham Lake, Massachusetts. *Author's collection.*

J.E. Copeland, "The Iceman," 1910. *Isabella and Carrol Walker Photograph Collection, Sargeant Memorial Collection, Norfolk Public Library.*

merchant Frederic Tudor, known as "Boston's Ice King." Tudor would cut blocks of ice from frozen ponds in Massachusetts in the winter and make runs in ships well-insulated with sawdust southward to the Caribbean, making ports of call along the way, including Norfolk.

"The scale of the operations was impressive," said Gavin Weightman in his book *The Frozen Water Trade*. "In 1847 nearly 52,000 tons of ice was shipped down the coast to twenty-eight different towns. To the established markets in New Orleans, Charleston and Savannah were added Washington D.C. Philadelphia, Mobile (Alabama), Key West (Florida), Norfolk (Virginia) and twenty more."

Suddenly, a new way of drinking opened up: iced drinks. "Before the Civil War of the 1860s…mint juleps…and other southern cocktails were made with ice shipped down from Boston," noted Weightman. In fact, ice was instrumental to juleps and other drinks like cobblers, fashionable during this era.

The *Alexandria Gazette* reported in its April 13, 1849 edition, "During the year 1847 the amount shipped from Boston to Southern ports in the United States was 51,887 tons [of ice]." The cost in southern ports, like New Orleans, varied greatly from a half cent to three cents per pound. At this point, Tudor no longer had a monopoly on the ice trade business.

Advances were made, and ice storage houses sprang up in towns, with ice delivery trucks making regular routes to homes and businesses later in the nineteenth century. Businesses and homes used iceboxes, insulated wooden boxes, to store the ice between deliveries or pickups.

During the Civil War, with ice from the North cut off, some Southerners turned to mechanical ice making, such as from machines produced by French engineer Ferdinand Carré. Increased advancements in artificial ice manufacturing in the late nineteenth and early twentieth centuries pushed out the traditional frozen water trade but not the love of iced cocktails.

THE MINT JULEP AND OTHER DRINKS

In many ways, the eighteenth century was a revolution in the way Virginia and the rest of America imbibed. Taverns that dotted the landscape of the Old Dominion became fewer and fewer, while grand hotels rose in towns from Norfolk and Virginia Beach northward to Richmond and Alexandria and westward as what was once the frontier in the Shenandoah Valley and beyond became established land. These hotels housed bars and saloons, with many more drinking options.

From America's greatest ally at the time, France, also came a revolutionary way of dining: the restaurant. These eating houses took hold at the turn of the new century, with the first opening in Norfolk, also offering bar areas that provided a very different imbibing experience than taverns had. Add to that the ability to have iced beverages year-round, plus the excitement of a new century in a new republic, and something grand was bound to happen. And it did: the cocktail.

Although there had been drinks of mixed spirits before, the cocktail combined certain elements in a standardized way that became an instant classic. And although there are many variations and interpretations, those many standards still hold true more than two hundred years later. "The earliest cocktails were about evolving consumption of spirits away from the neat pour, and toward mixed drinks," said sprits expert Kara Newman. Newman has penned several books on the subject, including *Cocktails with a Twist*. "That might have meant mixing with sugar, hot water (as in a toddy), or enriched with eggs or cream (as in flips or possess). It was also about evolving hospitality and presentation. How a drink was served was as important as how it was made....Today, I would say many of those same elements hold true. We have access to a much wider range of ingredients, but now more than ever cocktails are about hospitality (the bartending element) and presentation (hello, Instagram!)."

Cocktails themselves were developed over time, but the word *cocktail* doesn't seem to have been in use before 1798 or 1803, depending on which definition of the word and which source one subscribes to. Perhaps the most clear-cut definition came in 1806. It was then that the *Balance and Columbian Repository* editor Harry Croswell wrote in his Hudson, New York publication, "Cock-tail is a stimulating liquor, composed of spirits of any kind, sugar, water, and bitters—it is vulgarly called bittered sling."

It's not clear when the term became commonplace in the Commonwealth, but it began appearing in newspapers across Virginia, mostly in a negative manner from advocators of the temperance movement, early on. Keep in mind that many of the early temperance arguments encouraged sensible drinking of one or two beverages such as beer or wine, usually at a meal, and not the prohibition of alcohol completely.

Hard liquor, such as that found in cocktails, was another matter, as opined in an article in the May 2, 1827 issue of the *Phenix Gazette* in Alexandria: "[T]o make a pot-house of their bowel, and swill bitters, juleps, gin slings, cocktails, and a thousand other vulgar beverages from morn till night, in bar rooms and gin shops, argues as great a deficiency of physical taste as it does of common decency."

What many folks consider to be the oldest, most classic cocktail is the old fashioned, once known as a bittered sling. This drink is composed of a spirit (usually bourbon or rye whiskey), sugar, water and bitters and is spot-on in the definition from Harry Croswell. The cocktail may have appeared as early as the first quarter of the nineteenth century, but it had become well established by midcentury.

Although there were somewhat standard cocktail recipes about, it wasn't until 1862 that Professor Jerry Thomas published the first true cocktail recipe book, *How to Mix Drinks, or The Bon Vivant's Companion*—still a valuable guide in its own right.

One thing is obvious throughout Thomas's book: the role that ice plays. For the mint julep, ice is not only important—it is instrumental. It became as popular as it did because of the ice trade, as did other cocktails of the time, including the cobbler, fixes, fizzes, slings, the smash ("This beverage is simply a julep on a small plan," said Thomas) and sours. Punches were still popular, served with lots of ice. Also in vogue were highly iced temperance drinks, including lemonade.

> When the mint is in the liquor and
> its fragrance on the glass,
> It breathes a recollection that
> can never, never pass.
> —Clarence Ousley, "When the Mint Is in the Liquor"

The word *julep* itself has been used to describe things other than the frosty, minty drink that we know now. The Merriam-Webster Dictionary traces the etymology of the word to at least the fourteenth-century Middle English, which came from the Middle French, which came from Arabic, which came from the Persian *gulāb*, a combination of words meaning "rose water."

Early use of the word in England first described a syrup with a medicinal use and later a cordial to be consumed for pleasure, according to Richard Barksdale Harwell in his book *The Mint Julep*. "But the mint julep is truly American in its origin," Harwell noted.

Among the first notation of a mint julep was from a report by a traveler in a 1787 issue of *American Museum*, a magazine of the time. There the author wrote, "The Virginian rises in the morning, about six o'clock. He then drinks a julap, made of rum, water and sugar, but very strong." It's not surprising that it was made of rum, as this was about the time rum still had favoritism, although the new nation's palate was quickly turning toward whiskey. What's probably the most surprising thing is that a julep was thought of as a pre-breakfast drink.

It was also noted as such by Englishman John Davis, who penned *Travels of Four Years and a Half in the United States of America* in 1803. As a tutor on a Northern Virginia plantation, he recalled a story told to him by one of the plantation owner's slaves named Dick that among his tasks was mixing juleps for the plantation owner's son. "The first thing he did on getting out of bed was to call for a Julep," Davis quoted Dick as saying. As a footnote for readers in London, Davis explained that a julep is "[a] dram of spiritous liquor that has mint in it, taken by Virginians of a morning."

Jerry Thomas explained the julep in his *How to Mix Drinks, or The Bon Vivant's Companion*:

> *There are many varieties, such as those composed of claret, Madeira, &c; but the ingredients of the real mint julep are as follows. I learned how to make them, and succeeded pretty well.*
>
> *Put into a tumbler about a dozen sprigs of the tender shoots of mint, upon them put a spoonful of white sugar, and equal portions of peach and common brandy, so as it fill it up one-third, or perhaps a little less.*
>
> *Then take rasped or pounded ice, and fill up the tumbler. Epicures rub the lips of the tumbler with a piece of fresh pineapple, and the tumbler itself is very often incrusted outside with stalactites of ice. As the ice melts, you drink.*

An early recommendation for the mint julep came in the August 6, 1833 issue of Alexandria's *Phenix Gazette*: "Lee's Spring, or Rapidale Spring, about seven miles from Warrenton, Fauquier County (va.) is getting into great repute....Shacklett's...keeps a most excellent house...and moreover makes, it is generally admitted, the best mint julep that can be manufactured in the Old Dominion—which latter fact will be not slight recommendation, as times go, notwithstanding the temperance societies."

One place that quickly built a reputation for the quality of its mint juleps was a resort at White Sulphur Springs, simply referred to by the name of the town and healing waters where it was located. It later was known as The White, and later still The Old White. That part of Virginia became West Virginia when the state split in 1863, and today the resort is called The Greenbrier.

HARPER'S WEEKLY

A REMINISCENCE OF THE WHITE SULPHUR SPRINGS.—DRAWN BY C. B. REINHART.—[SEE PAGE 575.]

"A Reminiscence of the White Sulphur Springs," engraving from *Harper's Weekly*, August 1888, showing a young man sipping a mint julep. *Author's collection.*

The Greenbrier notes that its mint juleps were likely served at a tavern on the property as early as 1808 and that an account book from 1816 shows guests ordered the cocktail "at a cost of twenty-five cents per drink or three drinks for fifty cents."

The resort also reports that when Baltimore attorney John H.B. Latrobe visited in 1832, he wrote in his journal, "I saw here for the first time a hailstorm, that is to say, a mint julep made with a hailstorm around it. The drink is manufactured pretty much as usual and well filled with a quantity of ice chopped in small pieces, which is then put in shape of a fillet around the outside of the tumbler where it adheres like a ring of rock candy and forms an external icy application to your lower lip as you drink it, while the ice within the glass presses against your upper lip. It is nectar, they say, in this part of the country."

Confederate general Richard Taylor, son of Virginia-born president Zachary Taylor, also painted a florid word picture of a mint julep that he enjoyed at the home of distant relatives in Orange County in June 1862. He recalled it in his book *Destruction and Reconstruction: Personal Experiences of the Late War*. The description begins as a house slave is approaching him on the porch as breakfast is being served:

[He] *advanced holding a salver, on which rested a huge silver goblet filled with Virginia's nectar, mint julep. Quantities of cracked ice rattled refreshingly in the goblet; springs of fragrant mint peered above its broad rim; a mass of white sugar, too sweetly indolent to melt, rested on the mint; and, like rose buds on a snow bank, luscious strawberries crowned the sugar. Ah! that julep. Mars ne'er received such tipple from the hands of Ganymede.*

Taylor did not list the spirit used in the julep, but it was most likely at this point brandy or cognac, although folks were using a number of intoxicants as ingredients. Indeed, Thomas goes on to give recipes in his book for a mint julep made with "Jamaica rum," a brandy julep, a gin julep, a whiskey julep and a pineapple julep crafted with the fruit, gin and "sparkling Moselle."

In his *The Mint Julep Book*, Richard Barksdale Harwell noted, "After the Civil War, when home-grown ingredients were all most Southerners could afford, the bourbon mint julep gradually became the standard, and most Southerners today are surprised to learn that their regional drink was ever, or can be now, made with any other liquor."

MEET JOHN DABNEY

John Dabney was a culinary force to be reckoned with, a successful nineteenth-century caterer and bartender to the Virginia elite. He popularized the mint julep, even serving it to the Prince of Wales during a tour of the nation. He was also born a slave who worked and paid every penny to buy his and his wife's freedom.

Dabney was born around 1824 in Hanover County, north of Richmond, a slave to Cora Williamson DeJarnette, who hired the young man out to a relative, William Williamson, who trained him to be a jockey. Williamson, a horse breeder, was also a hotelier, and as Dabney grew older, his work shifted, working as a waiter in Hanover Junction (now Doswell) and also in Gordonsville, in Orange County.

"Williamson brought him to Richmond to tend bar at the Ballard House, his hotel. While tending bar, Dabney sought instruction from Jim Cook, the hotel's chef, and mastered cooking for the public," wrote food historian David S. Shields in his book *The Culinarian*. "Dabney's first fame attached to his abilities as a mixologist, more specifically, as a mixer of mint juleps."

By 1856, Dabney had married Elizabeth Foster, who was also born a slave, according to Philip J. Schwarz, writing for the *Dictionary of Virginia Biography* and *Encyclopedia Virginia*, and they had five sons and four daughters. Prior to her owner selling her out of Richmond, Dabney used "earnings from his bartending [and] enlisted the aid of sympathetic white men in purchasing his wife," said Schwarz. At this point, Dabney was also making payments to DeJarnette to purchase his own freedom.

Edward, Prince of Wales, who would become king of England with the passing of his mother, Queen Victoria, took his first tour of North America in 1860, including several stops in Virginia. While he was at the Exchange Hotel in Richmond, the *Times* in January 23, 1901, reported:

> *It was here that the Prince first made the acquaintance of a mint julep, and in this connection it is a matter of record that John Dabney, the barkeeper at the Exchange, received for this mint julep five five-dollar gold pieces.*
>
> *John, it would appear, viewed life from a commercial, rather than a sentimental vantage ground for he at once sold his five-dollar gold pieces for fifteen or twenty dollars each, thus securing for his julep some eighty or a hundred dollars. This probably holds the record for mint juleps.*

Perhaps that was used for his own freedom. In the end, Dabney was freed at the conclusion of the Civil War but still had a balance of $200. It was a promise he wanted to make good. "My master acted like a gentleman to me; he let me buy myself and my wife cheap; I owe him the money honestly, and I intend to pay it," noted an article in the September 26, 1866 issue of the *Alexandria Gazette* from the *Richmond Enquirer*. "John discharged the obligation in full. Such conduct evinces a regard for honor which would ennoble any man, and John will stand (and deservedly) higher than ever in the estimation of every Richmond gentleman."

Already with an outstanding regional reputation, Dabney's name grew nationally after the publicity. He was also able to go to a bank and borrow loans simply on his word and his word alone—always repaying his debt. "Dabney kept bar in several fashionable Richmond hotels before, during, and immediately after the Civil War," said Schwarz. He traveled across the state doing catering jobs at private functions and in people's homes, as well as bartending at popular resorts. Early in the 1870s, he opened his own restaurant. He seems to have relinquished management of his business in the early 1890s but worked until the week of his death, Schwarz noted.

The *Richmond Times* on June 8, 1900, reported Dabney's passing: "John Dabney, the well-known caterer and the celebrated julep maker, died at his residence, No. 1414 East Broad Street, at 9:30 o'clock last night....John

Dabney was for many years one of the best-known caterers in the South. He was for some time caterer at Old Sweet Springs and other famous resorts. He leaves a wife and five children. He was about seventy-five years of age."

In 2019, John Dabney was inducted into the Virginia Culinary Hall of Fame.

EFFECTS OF THE CIVIL WAR

The Civil War began on April 12, 1861, in South Carolina, with Virginia quickly seceding from the Union and Richmond being proclaimed the capital of the Confederacy. Many major campaigns were fought on Virginia soil until the war concluded with the surrender of Confederate general Robert E. Lee to Union general Ulysses S. Grant in the village of Appomattox Court House on May 9, 1865.

"During the Civil War, many distilleries in the south were destroyed," noted the Virginia Distillers Association. "Whiskey also became an important part of the lives of soldiers because it helped them cope with the hardships of the war."

For many, however, spirits in the South became difficult to find because many grain crops had been wiped out as a result of the war—or because the grains were needed for food for the war effort. Also, certain laws were put into place to funnel spirits from citizens to Confederate troops for medicinal uses, such as deadening pain and cleaning wounds due to antiseptic qualities. There were also Federal blockades of Confederate ports, preventing imports.

The *Alexandria Gazette* on October 17, 1862, reprinted an article from the *Richmond Whig* lamenting the "Popular Drinks" in "ye olden times" since alcohol was no longer available. "It applies elsewhere beside Richmond," it noted, adding:

> *The war has check the production, and Provost Marshals have arrested the sale of Whiskey. It cannot be obtained except as extravagant prices* [twelve dollars at fifteen per gallon], *and so the large majority of people, perforce, are dispensing with the use of the exhilarating fluid. Water is now the pop-prevailing drink! We believe it may be safely asserted that the quantity of water swallowed every day is more than double the quantity which formerly went down the throats of bibulous folks.*
>
> *People will not be satisfied with water. Every nation under the sun has some stimulant—the desire to imbibe it appears to be innate. As the supply of*

Detail of a drawing by Alfred R. Waud, May 5–8, 1864, "The Army Marching Past Todds Tavern," in unincorporated Spotsylvania County between the Battles of the Wilderness and Spotsylvania Court House during the Civil War. Taverns were centers of community and regional landmarks. *Library of Congress.*

Whiskey is nearly exhausted, and the production restricted by legislation, as well as by the exercise of military power, distillers are turning their attention to the apple crop (which is said to be abundant). The prospect is, that in a short time apple brandy will be the only liquor made and used in the South to any extent. Thus, we are likely to have an "Apple Brandy" era.

Despite grain shortages, some corn and other grains were crafted into distilled spirits in the civilian population. "Also one type of homemade alcoholic beverage that became popular in the South was made by the mixing one part corn syrup and/or molasses with three parts water and then fermenting it in a barrel," said Michael J. Varhola in *Life in Civil War America.*

Blockade runners also brought in whiskey and other items, primarily from Europe, but the cost was especially prohibitive. As the war dragged on, even whiskey that was obtainable legally was increasingly out of reach. The February 26, 1864 issue of the *Richmond Enquirer* reported, "Everything has an upward tendency. Yesterday, whiskey, which had been selling ten days ago for $90 per gallon, could not be bought at $120."

Just like Prohibition in the next century, restricting spirits did not prevent people from getting them—it just drove the trade underground. In the *Central Presbyterian of Richmond*'s February 25, 1864 issue, it was noted:

The Grand Jury of Rockbridge [County] *recently presented several distillers for making whiskey contrary to law. The first of these cases has just been tried. The offender was "no mean man"—and yet a jury of his peers, in despite of the efforts of "able counsel," found him guilty, fined him one hundred dollars, and the worthy Judge added to the fine the confiscation of his large and costly distillery, the sale of all the whiskey on hand at the Government price. And the incarceration of the Distiller's person in the county jail for thirty days.*

When the enormous wickedness of taking the bread out of the mouths of our famished soldiers and their families to make whiskey contrary to law is duly considered, every patriotic heart must overflow with gratitude to his Honor Judge Cambden and his Jury.

Drinking—legal and not—was true not only in the civilian world but also in the soldier's world. "Excessive drinking was a constant problem in both armies during the Civil War," wrote David A. Norris in his book *Forty-Rod, Blue Ruin & Oh Be Joyful: Civil War Alcohol Abuse* for Warfare History Network. He reported that the Norfolk Day-Book "complained that Confederate enlisted men and officers in the vicinity were drinking whiskey 'in quantities which would astonish the nerves of a cast-iron lamp-post, and of a quality which would destroy the digestive organs of an ostrich.'"

Plainly put, whiskey—whether legally obtained through some sort of issue or purchase or by bootlegging, smuggling or outright theft—was widely available to the Confederate soldier as a source of pleasure, although the quality was often suspect.

According to Varhola, some soldier slang for liquor included "bark juice," "o be joyful" and "red eye." The terms "bust head" and "pop skull" were reserved exclusively for cheap whiskey.

"Canteens were sometimes filled from stills located along the line of march in secluded mountain areas, and hospital patients purchased whiskey from nearby distillers and shipped it out to the camps in boxes marked 'Soldiers' Supplies.' Soldier correspondence is full of references to the heavy drinking," noted Horace Herndon Cunningham in *Doctors in Gray: The Confederate Medical Service.*

There were times, though, when commanders would issue a ration of whiskey for troop morale. A few drinks helped to commemorate a battlefield victory, a special occasion or a holiday, or just as a reward. When it wasn't doled out, though, desperate times called for desperate measures, it seems. Varhola noted that some Confederate soldiers made a bootleg liquor following a similar Northern recipe that included "bark juice, tar-water, turpentine, brown sugar, lamp-oil, and alcohol," sometimes throwing in a piece of raw meat and allowing it all to ferment for a month. It produced "an old and mellow taste," Varhola quoted a veteran as saying.

Still, spirits were also a vital commodity: whiskey was one of the many items used in field and hospital. They cleaned wounds, deadened pain and helped some to forget sorrows. But like soldiers who drank to forget the horrors of war, doctors did too. And like some soldiers, some doctors drank to excess. "The Surgeon General also kept his ear to the ground for news of misconduct in this respect, and on one occasion he called for an investigation of a report," wrote Cunningham. The report noted "that the Medical Officers on duty in Poplar Lawn Hospital [in Petersburg] are in the habit of drinking the hospital stimulants, whenever they think proper.… At Chimborazo [hospital], according to [nurse] Phoebe Pember, a drunken surgeon engaged in treating a patient with a crushed ankle placed the wrong leg in splints and thereby contributed to the soldier's death."

In the month or two following the end of the Civil War, it didn't take long for the spirits to begin flowing again, as evident by an abundance of advertisements in newspapers, such as this one in Richmond's *Commercial Bulletin* of July 1, 1865: John Clark & Company at 230 Main Street was promoting a "heavy stock of fine liquors" and "Last, but not least, a large assortment of Whiskeys, in bottles, cases and barrels. We particularly call attention to a consignment of 'Mountain Dew' Whiskey which we can sell as low as any in the market."

The Gay Nineties

The Gilded Age. The Gay Nineties. The Naughty Nineties.

Virginia, and all of America, had the Civil War and Reconstruction in its rear-view mirror, and for many, things looked bright as the nineteenth century came to an end. Even though the temperance movement had regathered strength, folks still loved their cocktails, and now the concept of a proper cocktail was firmly established. Opulent hotels and restaurants continued to open, with magnificent bars inside them. Many bars and saloons opened on their own, too, drawing crowds who wanted to enjoy life.

Dens of delectation illuminated in the latest technology, electricity, opened across the Commonwealth. A prime example of the opulence of the period was the Onyx Bar. It was called "a palace in Norfolk" and "a scene of rare brilliancy" in the headlines of the April 28, 1895 *Virginian-Pilot*.

Joseph Seelinger's Onyx Bar pulled in many folks through its doors, including a sitting president. "On the south side of [East] Main street [at 221 Main, near Church Street], just two doors east of the Purcell House,

George Thorpe is credited with crafting the first distilled spirits in what would become English-speaking America at Berkeley Plantation in 1620, as shown in this postcard. *Author's collection.*

RISING SUN TAVERN, FREDERICKSBURG, VA.   33502-C

The Rising Sun Tavern in Fredericksburg. Originally built as a home by the younger brother of George Washington, it became the Golden Eagle (or Eagle) Tavern in the 1790s. *Author's collection.*

Gadsby's Tavern in Alexandria has been a focal point of life in this Northern Virginia seaport since the opening of the circa 1785 tavern, the adjacent 1792 City Tavern and Hotel and the 1878 hotel addition. *Author's collection.*

Handcrafted ceramic jugs have historically been used for storage, transportation and sale of moonshine and other spirits, as with these two examples from the author's collection. *Author's collection.*

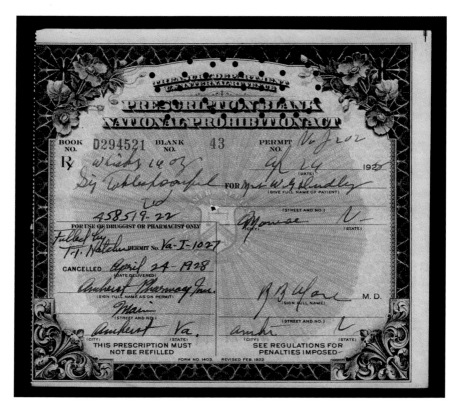

A doctor-written prescription (from Amherst) dated April 24, 1928, good for sixteen ounces of whiskey, with six tablespoons to be taken daily. *Author's collection.*

Bumbo cocktail with rustic crackers, farmer's cheese and fresh figs at Still Worldly Eclectic Tapas in Portsmouth. *Cocktail by Karl Dornemann, food styling by Stella Pomianek, photo by Lucas Pomianek; author's collection.*

Right: Bartender Karl Dornemann with a milk punch at Still Worldly Eclectic Tapas in Portsmouth. *Cocktail by Karl Dornemann, photo by Lucas Pomianek; author's collection.*

Below: Stone fence cocktail with molasses cookie at Still Worldly Eclectic Tapas in Portsmouth. *Cocktail by Karl Dornemann, food styling by Stella Pomianek, photo by Lucas Pomianek; author's collection.*

Above: Sangaree cocktail at Still Worldly Eclectic Tapas in Portsmouth. The vintage Colonial Williamsburg capitol building replica decanter is part of the author's culinary collection. *Cocktail by Karl Dornemann, photo by Lucas Pomianek; author's collection.*

Left: Cherry bounce cocktail at Still Worldly Eclectic Tapas in Portsmouth. *Cocktail by Karl Dornemann, photo by Lucas Pomianek; author's collection.*

A rye + ginger cocktail at Still Worldly Eclectic Tapas in Portsmouth. *Cocktail by Karl Dornemann, photo by Lucas Pomianek; author's collection.*

The Grover cocktail, named after President Grover Cleveland, at Still Worldly Eclectic Tapas in Portsmouth. *Cocktail by Karl Dornemann, photo by Lucas Pomianek; author's collection.*

A pitcher of mint juleps at Still Worldly Eclectic Tapas in Portsmouth. Vintage cardinal (Virginia's state bird) decanter and Bosman & Lohman peanut crate are parts of the author's culinary collection. *Cocktail by Karl Dornemann, photo by Lucas Pomianek; author's collection.*

The apple cobbler cocktail at Still Worldly Eclectic Tapas in Portsmouth. *Cocktail by Karl Dornemann, photo by Lucas Pomianek; author's collection.*

A spiked Teetotaler Lemonade at Still Worldly Eclectic Tapas in Portsmouth. *Cocktail by Karl Dornemann, photo by Lucas Pomianek; author's collection.*

A pitcher of Mid-Century Modern–ish Martinis and circa 1930s martini glasses from the author's culinary collection at Still Worldly Eclectic Tapas in Portsmouth. *Cocktail by Karl Dornemann, photo by Lucas Pomianek; author's collection.*

Above: Storm's Brewin' Cocktail, a fun take on a classic hurricane, at Still Worldly Eclectic Tapas in Portsmouth. *Cocktail by Karl Dornemann, photo by Lucas Pomianek; author's collection.*

Left: The COVID-19 pandemic–inspired Quarantini cocktail at Still Worldly Eclectic Tapas in Portsmouth. *Cocktail by Karl Dornemann, photo by Lucas Pomianek; author's collection.*

Bartender Karl Dornemann, who is also distiller at Reverend Spirits, holds up a late eighteenth-century pewter tavern mug that is part of the author's culinary collection at Still Worldly Eclectic Tapas in Portsmouth. *Photo by Lucas Pomianek; author's collection.*

Temperance leader Carrie Nation sold these hatchet pins to raise funds for her mission in the early twentieth century; displayed at Still Worldly Eclectic Tapas in Portsmouth. *Photo by Lucas Pomianek; author's collection.*

A trio of culinary artifacts from the author's culinary collections, displayed at Still Worldly Eclectic Tapas in Portsmouth, include a Prohibition-era flask attributed to Princess Anne County and early twentieth-century whiskey bottles from W.J. Tyson and H.C. Williams, both of Norfolk. *Photo by Lucas Pomianek; author's collection.*

A late nineteenth-century icepick from the Portsmouth Ice Delivery Corporation on display at Still Worldly Eclectic Tapas in Portsmouth from the author's culinary collection. *Photo by Lucas Pomianek; author's collection.*

Left: Bottle of Virginia-distilled Four Farthings Spiced Rum at Still Worldly Eclectic Tapas in Portsmouth. *Photo by Lucas Pomianek; author's collection.*

Below: Distiller testing product at A. Smith Bowman in Fredericksburg, the oldest distillery in Virginia. *A. Smith Bowman Distillery.*

Above: Tours are offered behind the scenes at A. Smith Bowman in Fredericksburg. *A. Smith Bowman Distillery.*

Left: Many distilleries have resident dogs who greet visitors, like Otto at Catoctin Creek Distillery. *Catoctin Creek Distillery.*

Left: The Virginia Distillers Association, known as Virginia Spirits, advocates for distilleries across the Commonwealth and offers a number of public education/tasting events annually. *Amy Ciarametaro.*

Below: Distiller Owen King moving barrels at Ironclad Distillery Company in Newport News. *Ironclad Distillery Company.*

Many of the offerings at the tasting room of Ironclad Distillery Company in Newport News. *Ironclad Distillery Company.*

A retail display at the distillery at Reverend Spirits in Norfolk in front of distillery equipment. *Reverend Spirits by David Schwartz.*

Left: A trio of offerings at the bar of Caiseal Beer & Spirits Company in Hampton includes vodka, the IPA Edition and gin. *Caiseal Beer & Spirits Company.*

Below: Barrel room at Reservoir Distillery in Richmond. *Reservoir Distillery.*

one comes upon a smooth granolithic sidewalk and his attention is at once drawn to the massive granite structure in Roman architecture, which towers above in majestic solidity and seemingly in defiance of the wear of time," recorded the newspaper.

The entrance, solid mahogany with plate glass panels, was illuminated with "electric lights and imitations candles, which are lighted with gas." Past the vestibule and "stepping inside the cafe you are as one transmitted to some foreign and ancient city, which to you seems as a dream. You think surely there can be nothing like this in Norfolk. You imagine yourself in one of the ancient temples."

Inside was a mosaic floor, with a half-million tile pieces, an embossed steel ceiling with skylight, electric ceiling fans and chandeliers made of crystal and burnished bronze, beveled glass mirrors on the walls and "the grand and massive bar fixture, which is of solid mahogany, pure Mexican onyx, and French plate mirrors. The wood work is magnificent. The panels and moldings are profusely carved by hand and the columns are all polished Mexican onyx.

Interior of the Onyx Bar, circa 1900, showing the large mirror that was reported by the *Virginian-Pilot* to have been smashed in a raid by temperance leader Carrie Nation. *Isabella and Carrol Walker Photograph Collection, Sargeant Memorial Collection, Norfolk Public Library.*

J. SEELINGER & SON   "THE ONYX"   411 E. Main St., NORFOLK, VA.

Interior of the Onyx, postcard, circa 1900. *Author's collection.*

There is no question as to this being the finest fixture of its kind in America. Between this fixture and the lunch counter, which is identically the same, is a beautiful refrigerator." There were private rooms as well as a billiard hall. "There is no word more appropriate in a description of this temple of mechanical art than grand, as it is truly a grand and imposing triumph of skilled labor and artistic taste," the report concluded.

Others felt the same way, and the bar was the place to see and be seen. Not everyone was a fan, however; prohibitionist Carrie Nation entered the bar, which she deemed "wicked," and threw a hatchet, shattering the barroom mirror, according to the *Virginian-Pilot*. When asked by a reporter about Nation's saloon-smashing crusade across the country, President Grover Cleveland said, "That is a social question upon which I am not qualified to speak," reported the March 13, 1902 *Richmond Times*. In fact, Cleveland was a fan of the Onyx and usually spent a few days as a guest of Seelinger's, where he ran the White House from the "old back room," as he described it, and slept in a room upstairs.

In the "Little White House" back room, according to a recollection by *Virginian-Pilot* reporter Harry P. Moore made in 1952, the president liked to enjoy cocktails of "whisky and ginger ale, or perhaps a concoction of his favorite whisky, mint, a slice of pineapple, and a piece of orange"—a

Exterior of the Onyx, circa 1961. *Isabella and Carrol Walker Photograph Collection, Sargeant Memorial Collection, Norfolk Public Library.*

mint julep—of which he said, "Unless the mint tickles your nose, it is not a real mint julep."

Moore noted that the Onyx was known nationally not just for its drinks but also for its eats. Often on the menu were duck and other waterfowl hunted in Back Bay. The Onyx "became widely known throughout the city by fastidious diners with whom cost was not a factor. In the gay days of Norfolk [it] was the center of fashionable gatherings, especially around the holiday season," noted Seelinger's obituary.

Joseph Seelinger's brothers also got in the business, with brother Anthony running his own saloon and brother Henry operating H. Seelinger's Stag Hotel and Ladies' and Gentleman's Café and Restaurant at 39 City Hall Avenue. Another brother, Steven, opened Steve Seelinger's Café at 10 Bank Street. Like others, the bars closed with the advent of Prohibition at midnight on October 31, 1916.

Seelinger died at his residence at 318 Mowbray Arch in Norfolk in 1939, and the Onyx changed hands, splitting into a hotel on the upper story and the Shangri La Oyster Bar on the ground floor. The building was demolished in February 1961 due to urban renewal efforts along the East Main Street area of the city.

RECIPES

A note on the revolution of drinking in the nineteenth century: three remarkable periods occurred in a short span of time from the Revolutionary War to Prohibition that defined imbibing and set many standards for today's enjoyment of adult beverages; the period or period-inspired recipes included here fall in one of three "ages" during this time.

In his essential book *Imbibe*, historian David Wondrich defined the first, the Archaic Age from 1783 until 1830, as "the formative years of American mixology, the tools were few, the recipes simple, the ingredients robust, and the mixology rough and ready." During this time, the cocktail began to emerge, such as the mint julep, and whiskey began to overtake rum as America's drink.

During the Baroque Age from 1830 until 1885, "Ice, combined with the American drinking public's ever-increasing preference for individual drinks made to order over things drunk communally out of bowls" was a new development, said Wondrich, and the bartender's job became more involved accordingly. Many methods and presentations were regarded as over the top.

From 1885 until 1920, the Classic Age saw, as Wondrich noted, "a new, lighter, and simpler breed of Cocktail." He added, "The definition of a Cocktail stretched to include ingredients like lemon juice, orange juice, pineapple juice, and the faddish and pink-making grenadine. By 1920, just about every technique and major ingredient known to modern mixology was in play."

APPLE COBBLER

A popular nineteenth-century cocktail, noted as perhaps the first shaken drink, the cobbler launched the popularity of ice and straws into popular culture. Comprising a spirit (such as rum), sugar, crushed ice—noted as "cobbles," where the drink drives its name from—and fruit, it was noted as early as 1842 and was popular through Prohibition.

In Thomas's 1862 bartender's guide, he listed recipes for cobblers made from a number of wines, including claret, Catawba, champagne, hock, sauterne and sherry. He also crafted a whiskey cobbler, which is our inspiration. In his book, he wrote, "Like the julep, this delicious potation is an American invention, although it is now a favorite in all warm climates. The 'cobbler' does not require much skill in compounding, but to make it acceptable to the eye, as well as to the palate, it is necessary to display some taste in ornamenting the glass after the beverage is made…to suit an epicure."

Virginia knows apples. More than one hundred commercial orchards cover some sixteen thousand acres of land in the state, producing 5 to 6 million bushels annually. Following the warm days of summer and during the increasingly cool nights of early autumn, apples reach their peak flavor. In Virginia, harvest begins in July and runs through early November, with the majority of the crop going to market in September and October.

According to the Virginia Apple Board, some of Virginia's most prominent apples include Fuji, Gala, Ginger Gold, Golden Delicious, Granny Smith, Jonathan, Red Delicious, Rome, Stayman, Winesap and York.

A note for the recipe following: you can omit the applejack/apple brandy and increase the whiskey by one ounce for a pure whiskey cobbler, and you can garnish with seasonal fruit or an orange slice, as Thomas would have done.

2 ounces whiskey
1 ounce applejack or apple brandy, such as Laird's
1 ounce simple syrup
club soda, optional
apple wedge
mint

Fill an old fashioned glass with crushed ice and pour in the whiskey, applejack and simple syrup; stir well and, optionally, top off with club soda. Garnish with a thin wedge of apple and fresh mint sprig and serve with an ecologically friendly straw. Yields 1 cocktail.

GIN FIX

The fix was a refreshing cocktail of the nineteenth century that, like many drinks of the era, capitalized on using lots of ice. In Jerry Thomas's indispensable 1862 recipe book *How to Mix Drinks, or The Bon Vivant's Companion*, he gave guidelines on crafting a brandy fix and a gin fix. You could also use other spirits in this drink, such as whiskey—have fun and experiment.

For the gin fix, Thomas noted to use a small bar glass and "fill two-thirds full of shaved ice." From there you add "1 table-spoonful of sugar, ½ of a lemon, ½ a wine-glass of water, [and] 1 wine glass of gin." He noted to "[s]tir with a spoon, and ornament the top with fruits in season."

For fruits of the season to garnish the cocktail, we refer to the invaluable Virginia Grown website from the Virginia Department of Agriculture and Consumer Services and select strawberries in the spring; blackberries, blueberries and raspberries in the early summer; watermelon in the late summer; and apples and pears in the autumn and winter.

Here is our take on Professor Thomas's gin fix.

2 ounces gin
2 teaspoons fresh lemon juice
1 teaspoon water
1 teaspoon superfine sugar

Fill an old fashioned glass about three-fourths full shaved ice. Add the gin, lemon juice, water and sugar. Garnish with seasonal fruits and serve with an ecologically friendly straw. Yields 1 cocktail.

THE VIRGINIA FIZZ

The fizz is variation on a sour cocktail but is crafted with the addition of carbonated water to give fizz, hence its signature name. It did not appear in earlier versions of Thomas's bartending guide, but there were four variations in the 1876 edition, where it was spelled "fiz." From the late nineteenth century on, it grew in popularity, particularly the gin fizz. There are several variations of a gin fizz, with the Ramos Gin Fizz and the Sloe Gin Fizz being the better known. Fizzes can be made with alcohol other than gin, such as rum and whiskey, as with ours.

Our fizz takes another twist by incorporating strawberries. Historian George Percy wrote, not long after the first landing at Cape Henry on April 26, 1607, "Going a little further we came into a plat of ground full of fine and beautifull Strawberries, foure times bigger and better than ours in England."

Berries grew wild in Virginia Beach and across Coastal Virginia, and Percy, Captain Christopher Newport, bon vivant John Smith and others noted the abundance—and deliciousness—of the fruit. Soon, settlers began to cultivate strawberries and ship the plants back to England. There, they were prized for their flavor and size. In fact, *Fragaria virginiana*, the Virginia strawberry, was one of two species that were hybridized to create the domestic garden strawberry.

3–4 fresh strawberries
½ teaspoon superfine sugar
3 ounces Virginia whiskey
1 ounce fresh squeezed lemon juice
club soda
1 whole strawberry

To prepare the strawberries, wash, hull and dice the strawberries. Add to an old fashioned glass.

To prepare the cocktail, add sugar on top of strawberries and muddle until berries are well mashed. Add whiskey and lemon juice and stir until sugar is dissolved. Add ice cubes about three-fourths up the side of the glass and top with club soda. Garnish with a whole strawberry.

Optionally, you can substitute strawberries for other berries—such as blueberries, blackberries or raspberries—or omit the berries completely. Yields 1 cocktail.

THE GROVER

As president, Grover Cleveland liked to visit his friend Joseph Seelinger and go duck hunting in Back Bay in Princess Anne County, now in present-day Virginia Beach. He slept in a room upstairs in Seelinger's celebrated Onyx Bar (which opened in Norfolk in 1895) and conducted national affairs in the "Little White House" in a back room. He enjoyed mint juleps and a drink of his own concoction consisting of whiskey and ginger ale. This cocktail is inspired by the twenty-second—and twenty-fourth—American commander in chief.

1 ½ ounces rye whiskey
dash or two Angostura or orange bitters
4 ounces ginger ale
orange wedge

Fill a tall glass with ice. Add whiskey and a dash or two of Angostura bitters, top off with ginger ale and stir. Garnish with a wedge of orange. Yields 1 cocktail.

ESSENTIALS FOR A MINT JULEP

Whether you want a management mint julep or a mint julep that is monumental, there are some basics that hold true. Follow these essentials and you can't go wrong.

INGREDIENTS
GARNISH: *Any garnishes you use in addition to mint should be the freshest possible and completely edible, such as cherries, pineapple chunks on skewers, pineapple wedges, whole or halved strawberries, whole edible flowers like orchids or pansies or petals from a rose. A note on use of flowers: Make sure they have been grown without use of any pesticides.*

ICE: *The ice should always be crushed or shaved, never cubed. It is acceptable to place cubes in a cloth bag (or even a clean pillow case), fold over several times and beat it like it owes you money until it is broken up into very small pieces.*

MINT: *Use the freshest mint possible and cut very long stems to place deep within the cup. Gently wash the mint before use and pat dry with paper towels.*

SUGAR: *Always use superfine sugar and never granulated sugar—it will dissolve better.*

SPIRITS: *While bourbon is today's standard, try other whiskeys like rye or experiment with brandy, gin or rum. Just make sure it is distilled in Virginia.*

EQUIPMENT

CUP: *The cup should be pewter or silver and made specifically for juleps, or a similar cup or goblet. You can also use copper, such as a mule mug. Do not use glass.*

STRAW: *Use a metal straw if possible to conduct the cold and to be friendlier to the environment. Paper straws are acceptable; if they are used, cut them short so that the nose goes down deep into the bouquet of mint.*

TRAY: *A pewter or silver tray is a must for serving the juleps to your guests. It also eliminates getting any pesky fingerprints on the cups.*

Method

Pre-chill the cup: Pack the cups with crushed/shaved ice about 30 minutes before preparing the drinks and then discard. Use the cup immediately afterward. This prevents the ice in the drink from melting too quickly.

Pack the mint: Both in with the ice and press as much down into the top of the ice as possible to fully fragrant the drink.

Holding the cup: Hold very carefully as to not get any fingerprints on the cup once it starts becoming frosty. Seriously.

A MOST MARVELOUS MINT JULEP

In the 1906 *The New Lucile Cook Book*, General Dabney H. Maury of Richmond related John Dabney's mint julep recipe just a few years after the bartender's passing, seemingly from the lips of the master himself: "Crushed ice, as much as you can pack it in, and sugar, mint, bruised and put in with the ice, then your good whiskey, and the top surmounted by more mint, a strawberry, a cherry, a slice of pineapple, or, as John expressed it, 'any other fixings you like.'"

Note: Follow the "Essentials for a Mint Julep" above for A Most Marvelous Mint Julep to put to your lips.

6–8 fresh mint leaves
1 ½ teaspoons superfine sugar
3 ounces Virginia bourbon
confectioners' sugar
mint sprigs
pineapple wedge

In a chilled julep or other pewter or silver cup, or in a mule or other copper mug, add mint leaves, sugar and a slash of water and muddle. Pack the cup/mug with crushed or shaved ice and pour on bourbon. Sprinkle a very generous amount of confectioners' sugar and press multiple sprigs of fresh mint into the ice. Garnish with a pineapple wedge. Serve with an ecologically friendly straw.

AN OLD FASHIONED SLING

The sling is an old cocktail—in fact, an old fashioned cocktail. This classic drink, which evolved in the late nineteenth century into the drink we know today, had its origins early and was described in 1806 in the Hudson, New York publication the *Balance and Columbian Repository* when editor Harry Croswell wrote, "Cock-tail is a stimulating liquor, composed of spirits of any kind, sugar, water, and bitters—it is vulgarly called bittered sling." It's an individual serving of punch, of sort, without the fruit—except for garnish.

According to the online drinking culture magazine *Difford's Guide*, the word *sling* comes from the German *schlingen*, meaning "to swallow." It notes that slings are similar to toddies, although modern-day toddies are never served cold, where slings can be. In fact, Jerry Thomas in his bartending guide lists toddies and slings together. The book has recipes for three slings: brandy sling, hot whiskey sling and gin sling.

Slings were mentioned in the January 25, 1856 issue of the *Alexandria Gazette*, reporting on the latest story from Charles Dickens, "The Holly-Tree," which it noted was "his own…experiences [in an] American inn, depicted with too much truth, as well as just a trifle too much sarcasm." Dickens wrote of standing "in the bar-rooms thereof, taking my evening cobbler, julep, sling, or cocktail" each evening. Perhaps he enjoyed an old fashioned.

1 sugar cube
3 dashes Angostura or orange bitters
orange slice
3 ounces bourbon
club soda, optionally
orange peel
maraschino cherry

In the bottom of an old fashioned glass, add the sugar cube and drop on bitters. Add orange slice and muddle. Add several ice cubes and bourbon then stir well. Add a splash of soda water, optionally. Garnish with an orange peel and cherry. Yields 1 cocktail.

WHISKEY SMASH

The smash is a type of julep. In fact, in his *How to Mix Drinks*, Jerry Thomas wrote, "This beverage is simply a julep on a small plan." The bartender takes fresh ingredients such as fruit and herbs, smashes them and serves them in a glass with sugar or simple syrup and a spirit, often bourbon or rye. It is then packed with crushed or shaved ice.

One wonders what spirit was served up by I. Rammel, who showcased the drink in an advertisement in the March 5, 1877 edition of the *Alexandria*

Gazette: "IF YOU WANT A SMASH OR A MINT JULEP, OR ANY DRINK, WHY RAMMEL'S MARKET SPACE IS the only place to get them pure. The BEST OF LIQUORS, WINES and CIGARS always on hand."

In his guide, Thomas gave recipes for a brandy smash, gin smash and whiskey smash, which is very julep-like, without much of the pomp and circumstance. More updated versions, like ours, include a citrus pop, usually from lemon.

2–3 lemon wedges
6–8 fresh mint leaves
1 tablespoon simple syrup
3 ounces Virginia whiskey
club soda, optional
mint sprigs

In an old fashioned glass, add lemon wedges, mint leaves and simple syrup and muddle, juicing the lemon and bruising the mint. Fill the glass halfway with crushed or shaved ice, add the whiskey and stir. Fill the glass with more crushed or shaved ice and top with a splash of soda water if desired. Garnish with a fresh mint sprig and serve with an ecologically friendly straw. Yields 1 cocktail.

GIN RICKEY

A favorite drink of the nineteenth century, this cocktail has ties to Shoomaker's bar in Washington, D.C., and Democratic lobbyist Colonel Joe Rickey in the 1880s. It continued to gain popularity into the next century.

This highball cocktail is made with gin or bourbon (the original was crafted with bourbon), half a lime squeezed and dropped in the glass and carbonated water. Seldom is sugar added to a rickey, allowing for a pleasant tartness. By the 1890s, gin had become the favored spirit in the cocktail over bourbon. There are a number of variations, including one made with rum. The Cuban classic mojito is also related, crafted with lime, mint, rum, sugar and soda water.

The refreshing effects of a rickey were promoted in an advertisement in the June 22, 1905 (Richmond) *Times Dispatch* by the Hotel Lawrence

Café: "Yes, It Is Hot All Right! But suppose you were under the fans at Hotel Lawrence Cafe drinking a Gin Rickey, Mint Julep, High Bail, or Cold Bottle (any brand) Beer, don't you think you would cool off some? Twelfth and Main."

2 ounces Virginia gin
juice of one fresh squeezed lime
club soda
lime wedge

Fill a highball glass with ice. Add gin and lime juice. Top with soda water and garnish with a lime wedge. Yields 1 drink.

WHISKEY SOUR

Sours are a wide and varied family of cocktails, dating back to at least the mid-nineteenth century—although, if you squint, it isn't too difficult to see a connection with grog, the seafaring standard of rum and water for more than one hundred years by that point.

Jerry Thomas had two recipes in his 1862 bartending guide, one for a brandy sour and one for a gin sour, wrapping them up on the same page as fixes. Generally, the basic elements from Thomas's time to now stay the game: a spirit, citrus like lemon or lime juice and a sweetener like simple syrup. Other sweeteners include amaretto as in an amaretto sour, fruit juices like grenadine and orange juice in the whiskey sour variation Ward 8 or an orange liqueur as in a margarita.

Whiskey sours outpaced the brandy and gin sour. In the August 22, 1872 (Richmond) *Daily Dispatch*, an all-points bulletin was put out on a bank robber fitting the description of having a "very red face, a cast in one of his eyes, black hair, and always…clean shaven. He also dressed well, and was a great lover of 'whiskey sour,' or as the drink at this season of the year is more generally known, 'lime punch.'"

By the next year, the drink was among several that Europeans were enjoying, noted the July 12, 1873 *Alexandria Gazette*: "The following is a list of the plain American drinks that our German friends are beginning to learn to like, which are served up smothered in crushed ice." About fifty drinks were mentioned, with the end of the tally reading, "whiskey cocktail, whiskey punch, whiskey julep…whiskey sling, whiskey smash, whiskey sour."

Note: Craft this drink in a tall glass and add club soda and you end up with a Collins cocktail, regardless of the spirit.

2 ounces Virginia whiskey
1 teaspoon fresh lemon juice
½ teaspoon superfine sugar
1 orange slice
1 maraschino cherry

Fill an old fashioned glass about three-fourths with ice cubes; add whiskey, lemon juice and sugar and stir until sugar is dissolved. Garnish with orange slice and cherry. Yields 1 drink. Note: Our recipe omits the traditional use of egg whites.

TEETOTALER LEMONADE

Oh, those darn teetotalers, trying to push the temperance movement and make everyone drink lemonade instead of limoncello. Well, you know what they say: everything in moderation—even moderation.

The idea of alcohol prohibition was around in Virginia and other American colonies even before the Revolutionary War, but just as the eighteenth century ended, a momentum began to build. At first, some alcohol was permissible, such as beer or wine, especially with a meal. But as the nineteenth century progressed, the temperance movement became stricter, looking to restrict all forms of boozy beverages.

Here's something those do-gooders may have enjoyed while trying to kill the joy of others. If you are feeling impish, you can spike yours and no one will ever know.

Honey Syrup Ingredients
1 cup honey
1 cup water

Lemonade Ingredients
1 cup fresh squeezed lemon juice
2–3 cups cold water
lemon wedges
mint sprigs
rum, vodka or whiskey (optional)

To make the honey syrup, in a small saucepan add honey and water and bring to a boil, stirring frequently. Reduce to a simmer and stir frequently until honey has dissolved. Remove from stove and cool. Add to a sealable glass jar and refrigerate until use, up to 1 month.

To make the lemonade, in a large pitcher add the honey syrup, lemon juice and two cups of cold water and stir. Taste; add up to one more cup of water if you wish but know that the added ice will also dilute the beverage. Refrigerate 45 minutes until chilled. Serve with ice, garnished with lemon wedges and a sprig of mint.

To make it not so innocent, if you wish, add 1 to 2 ounces of Virginia rum, vodka or whiskey to the iced glass before pouring in the lemonade. Once lemonade is added, stir and garnish. Yields 4–6 servings.

TOM & JERRY

"An early-1800s classic, the Tom and Jerry is made with a cake-like egg batter that's combined with brandy and rum and topped with warm milk. It's a kissing cousin of eggnog, only hot," wrote Megan Krigbaum for the online magazine *Punch*. It's been likened to drinking a sugar cookie—a very, very boozy sugar cookie.

The Tom & Jerry may have originated as early as 1821, although some attribute it to midcentury bartender Jerry Thomas. In fact, in Thomas's bartending guide, he said that his name, Jerry Thomas, is used synonymously with the drink, as is the name Copenhagen.

So popular was the Tom & Jerry that it was even served in its own bowl, often emblazoned with the words "Tom & Jerry" on it, making it perhaps the first drink to have its own serving piece specifically crafted for it. Thomas gave guidelines in his book for serving individual customers from the bowl into a "small bar glass." The drink remained popular into the early twentieth century, with interest waning and then picking back up for a while in the 1940s.

Unlike eggnog, which can be served hot or cold, the Tom & Jerry is always served hot.

Batter Ingredients
6 eggs, separated
¼ teaspoon sea salt
½ teaspoon pure vanilla extract
1 cup unsalted butter at room temperature
6 cups confectioners' sugar
½ teaspoon ground allspice
½ teaspoon ground cinnamon
½ teaspoon ground cloves
½ teaspoon ground nutmeg

Cocktail Ingredients
spiced rum, such as Four Farthing Spiced Rum
whole cinnamon sticks
freshly grated nutmeg

To make the batter, in a large glass mixing bowl combine egg whites and salt and beat until stiff peaks form; set aside. In a separate large glass mixing bowl combine egg yolks with vanilla extract and beat until combined; set aside. In a separate large mixing bowl combine butter with 1 cup of sugar at a time, beating to incorporate until all sugar is added and mixture is fluffy and light.

To the butter mixture, add the egg yolks and mix to combine. Add allspice, cinnamon, cloves and nutmeg and mix to combine. Add the egg whites and fold in until everything is incorporated. Cover and refrigerate until ready to use. Batter will keep, refrigerated, for 2–3 days.

To make the cocktail, pour boiling water into a coffee mug and let sit for 3–5 minutes. Discard water and add 2–3 ounces of spiced rum. Add 1–2 heaping tablespoons of batter and pour over 4 ounces of hot milk. Stir to mix. Garnish with a cinnamon stick and a sprinkle of freshly grated nutmeg. Yields 12–18 servings.

Chapter 4

THE TWENTIETH CENTURY

STORM ON THE HORIZON

Although the Gay Nineties ushered in a new century and new reasons for hope, many barkeeps, distillers and others in the spirits trade had reason to temper that hope with caution.

The temperance movement continued to build strength, and it seemed that Virginia, if not the whole country, was getting closer and closer to a complete prohibition of alcoholic beverages. Of course, that didn't mean folks wouldn't be able to get them—they would just be underground and, as such, more expensive. The illicit alcohol trade was thriving—located mostly in rural areas where smoky pots could bubble away at mash and create clear corn liquor so strong it earned its name white lightning. And it would continue.

The end of Prohibition would lead right into tensions abroad for the second time in the century as the Commonwealth and the rest of the nation built up to World War II. Following the war, an era of prosperity settled in, and folks seemed to discover the joy of cocktails all over again, even if some of the drinks were monstrous. Virginians started the next century with a renewed patriotism and new thirst for local spirits.

Anti-Saloon League propaganda postcard, circa 1900. *Author's collection.*

VIRGINIA: THE MOONSHINE CAPITAL

Moonshine has been part of Virginia's heritage for four centuries, when the first corn liquor came off early stills such as colonist George Thorpe's at Berkeley Plantation in 1620. His, a predecessor to bourbon, was a type of white dog, a clear, potent drink that was imbibed without any barrel aging.

It was this drink that proliferated as Virginia's frontier opened up across the Blue Ridge and beyond, into the Shenandoah Valley, the Allegheny Mountains and the vastness that would later break off and become such states as Kentucky and West Virginia. Far from the ports of Coastal Virginia, settlers had to be almost completely self-sufficient in eats and drinks.

Corn grew abundantly in the frontier, and the legacy of crafting a liquor based on the grain flourished. Once additional Scotch-Irish pioneers laid their claim to the land alongside the English, new distilling techniques were introduced and others improved. Corn liquor solved the problem of being isolated in the mountainous regions too: for farmers, it was easier to transport harvested crops to market. Roads were narrow and, at times, virtually nonexistent. Wagons loaded down with corn and other grains would have a difficult time traversing passages into towns, but if the corn, rye and the like were liquid, it made them easier to transport as well as more profitable. Plus, the whiskey was less likely to go bad or spoil in storage, transportation and distribution than the raw grain product itself.

'Shine is relatively easy to make. The grains are broken down in water, and sugar and a combination of other ingredients like malt and yeast are added and created into a mash. The fermented mash (called the "beer" or "teedum") is put in a pot and heated. This removes the alcohol from the mash as it turns it into a vapor. The vapor coils around and, as it is cooled, turns back into a liquid and is collected in another pot. The un-aged product is sold as is.

The product was noted as being strong, as country singer George Jones noted in his 1959 song "White Lightning":

> *Well I asked my old pappy why he called his brew*
> *White lightnin stead of mountain dew.*
> *I took a little sip and right away I knew*
> *As my eyes bugged out and my face turned blue.*
> *Lightnin' started flashin thunder started clashin',*
> *Whew white lightnin'*

760 A TYPICAL MOONSHINE STILL IN THE HEART OF THE MOUNTAINS

This postcard proclaims "A Typical Moonshine Still in the Heart of the Mountains," circa 1950. *Author's collection.*

So, moonshine was well established before similar grain distillates began being aged in charred wooden barrels around the end of the eighteenth century, giving them the classic mellow flavor and amber appearance we associate with bourbons and ryes today.

Moonshine and other illicit drinks saw a surge during the Civil War, especially in Virginia and the American South, as the Union blocked ports, preventing the importation of spirits from international markets. Also, the Confederate government confiscated and rounded up alcoholic beverages to be used in the war effort, principally for analgesic and antiseptic needs at the frontline and in hospitals. Sale to the general public was prohibited.

In addition, Southern cities and towns under Union siege had alcohol confiscated and its sale prohibited. As the Union moved across the Confederacy, it also destroyed distilleries and many crops, including grain crops. It all created a ready opportunity for alcohol to be sold on the black market.

That pattern repeated itself about a half century later in 1916 as Prohibition became law in Virginia and later across the nation in 1920. There is still plenty of illegal moonshine being made in Virginia and throughout America, but you can also find your fair share of legally produced canned heat, hooch, 'shine and white lightning.

The term *moonshine* goes back to the early fifteenth century, and it seems to have begun being used as a description for illicit or smuggled spirits from 1785, according to the Online Etymology Dictionary. Roots of the word all meet at the same convergence. The first is simply the idea that someone is doing something, most likely covert, under the cover of darkness at night. Along those lines is that it comes from the fires of stills that burn away to create the liquor, and the smoke cannot be seen in the night sky by law enforcement as it would during the day.

A more specific tale is that of the moonrakers, an English tale of two Wiltshire men from 1787. As the story goes, the men were smuggling expensive brandy at night in a cask strapped to the back of their donkey. As they neared a river crossing, the donkey bolted, running away and throwing the cask into the water.

The men each grabbed a rake and began trying to fish the brandy from the river. About that time, a tax man came upon them and asked them what they were doing. One of the men saw his and his friend's reflection as they were raking across the moonlight shining across the surface of the water. "We are here, trying to rake up the cheese from the moon," he told the tax man, who doubled over in laughter and moved on.

The etymology dictionary says that the term *moonshine* began seeing use in 1829; research indicates that it doesn't appear to have been in widespread use in Virginia until after the Civil War. A descriptive word in favor in the eighteenth and nineteenth centuries was *forty-rod*, which as Derek Nelson in his *Moonshiners, Bootleggers & Rumrunners*, notes, "suggests how far you were removed from reality, or the distance it makes you run before you pass out."

Another was "mountain dew," which inspired the name of the current soft drink. A phrase that made its way over from Ireland and Scotland, it was quickly applied, especially in the mountainous regions of Virginia and the rest of Appalachia with the influence of immigrants from those countries.

Although later the brand name of a whiskey, the name "mountain dew" was sanctioned as a generic descriptor in the 1909 "Decisions of the Commissioner of Patents" from the U.S. Supreme Court by quoting several authoritative sources. Among those was the 1895 edition of the *Standard Dictionary*, which called mountain dew "illicitly-distilled whisky; so called from being very commonly made among the mountains."

In the May 28, 1868 issue of the *Richmond Daily Dispatch*, an advertisement ran promoting the "MOUNTAIN DEW COCKTAIL." It noted that bartender "CHARLEY LOEHR, at HENRY SCHOTT'S 'LAYFAYETTE SALOON' [established in 1842 by Louis Rueger, Esq.], CORNER OF NINTH AND BANK STREETS, prepares this delicious COCKTAIL from the celebrated 'W. Wallace's pure Mountain Dew Whiskey.'" It also noted that it was sold by the drink, bottle, gallon or barrel.

Wallace tootled its own horn a year later in the September 25, 1869 issue of the *Richmond Daily Dispatch*: "William Wallace Sons, wholesale dealers in LIQUORS, and proprietors of the celebrated 'MOUNTAIN DEW,' have in store and in bond a large assortments of VIRGINIA MOUNTAIN WHISKEYS, much of which have been held for upwards of TWO YEARS."

The advertisement concluded with: "Their 'MOUNTAIN DEW' is known from Canada to Florida and from Cuba to California. It is a favorite wherever brought into competition with the best distillations of the North, South, and West."

In the September 4, 1901 issue of the *Lexington (VA) Gazette*, an advertisement for the L. Lazarus Company, of Lynchburg, called itself "the largest liquor house in southwest, Virginia." Among a list of other items for sale was "Mountain Dew, smooth and full bodied rye, only $2.00 per gallon."

Later still, it was immortalized in the 1928 Appalachian folk song "Good Old Mountain Dew," by Bascom Lamar Lunsford and Scotty Wiseman, with lyrics that included:

> *Oh they call it that ole mountain dew*
> *And them that refuse it are few*
> *I'll shut up my mug if you fill up my jub*
> *With some good ole mountain dew.*

The song has been recorded by the likes of Glen Campbell and Willie Nelson.

Here are some other terms for moonshine that have developed over the course of time, including some in use currently:

"alky": shortened from the word *alcohol*.

"bootleg": referring to the way folks would often sneak flasks of alcohol in the leg of their boot.

"booze": a generic term for alcohol as a whole.

"canned heat": so named because of the hot properties of the spirit due to its high alcohol content, as well as the volatile nature of imbibing moonshine.

"coffin varnish": a term popularized during Prohibition, referring to alcohol of inferior quality.

"corn squeezin'" (sometimes "corn squeezins"): a term that refers to the grain used in moonshine.

"embalming fluid": a term popularized during Prohibition, referring to alcohol of inferior quality.

"hooch": a generic term for alcohol, particularly that of inferior quality.

"likker": a generic term for alcohol pronounced similar to *liquor* but quicker and more emphasis on the *q* as a *k*.

"medicine" (sometimes "cough medicine" or "cough syrup"): a term often used by a teetotaler to excuse the occasional indiscretion.

"moon": moonshine, simply shortened.

"pop skull": a phrase used in general for poorer-quality spirits, referencing hangover headaches from too much drinking.

"the recipe" (sometimes the "family recipe"): an Old Virginia term showing the reverence for each family's own 'shine method.

"rotgut": a term popularized during Prohibition, referring to alcohol of inferior quality.

"sauce": a generic term for alcohol as a whole.

"'shine": moonshine, simply shortened.

"white dog" (sometimes "white mule"): so named because the liquid is white and so strong it either bites you like a dog or kicks you like a mule.

"white lightning": like white dog, so named because the liquid is white and so strong it feels like you are struck by lightning.

Not a synonym per se, but you'll hear reference to "sugar shine," which is a fast and cheap way of making moonshine, foregoing corn for white and/or brown sugar (and perhaps a high-sugar fruit like raisins). Molasses could also be used.

With such a rich, long-standing history, Virginia's role as the "Moonshine Capital" goes undisputed. And the empirical seat of power for the capital is Franklin and surrounding counties. Franklin County itself, named for Benjamin Franklin, was formed in 1785 from Henry and Bedford Counties and added to from Patrick County. It's here in the rolling Blue Ridge foothills, nestled just southwest of Lynchburg and just southeast of Roanoke, that the national spotlight of moonshine and moonshining illuminated brightly in the early twentieth century.

The October 14, 1880 issue of the *Richmond Daily Dispatch* described the region: "The top of Bull mountain, in Patrick [County], [the] best moonshine whiskey is distilled from the dews of the morning, the fruits of the luscious orchards, and flaming grain of the fields."

Many distillers were operating legally—with government licensing and paying taxes—through much of the 1800s, save the occasional smaller operation still tucked in the woods. But that changed at the century as the temperance movement ramped up. Virginia as a whole enacted prohibition in 1916, four full years before it went nationwide. However, many counties across the state went dry—or prohibited the consumption and/or sale of alcohol—before the statewide ban.

And so the illicit alcohol trade began ramping up, and the words *bootlegging* and *moonshining* became near commonplace. During Prohibition, Franklin County gained a reputation for being ground zero for illicit alcohol trade when *Liberty* magazine writer Sherwood Anderson called it the "wettest county in the world" while coving the 1935 "Great Moonshine Conspiracy Trial." Although this trade had a dark side with organized criminal elements, moonshining also created a type of relatable underdog, such as during the Whiskey Rebellion. It also begat another legacy: NASCAR.

At the end of the day, Virginians still have that free spirit in them that set them apart from Mother England that likes things unregulated and untethered. Moonshine fulfills that bill. But purchasing moonshine made illegally isn't something most folks want to do, and today there is plenty of legal moonshine to be had in Virginia. Two of the pioneers on legal 'shine in the state are Chuck and Jeanette Miller of Belmont Farm Distillery in Culpeper. Coming from a family of moonshiners, the couple turned their farm into the distillery in 1988, making it the first craft whiskey distillery in the United States. Their first product was Virginia Lightning, a clear corn spirit crafted in a three-thousand-gallon copper pot still, built following Prohibition in 1933. The 100 proof Virginia Lightning began being sold in ABC stores across the commonwealth in 1989 and still is today.

Like with many other moonshine traditions, Belmont Farm Distillery also offers fruit-flavored moonshine—such as apple pie, cherry and peach—to appeal to different palates. A more unusual product is Virginia Lightning Butterscotch, noted with flavors of caramel and toffee; the Millers added, "Don't blame us if you feel the urge to add it to your early morning joe or the office coffee pot."

Another boost to legal hooch happened in 2013 when brothers-in-law Vince Riggi and Brian Marks founded Belle Isle Craft Spirits in Richmond and produced a premium moonshine "that offers all the versatility of vodka but with a bit more character and a smoother finish," according to an article on the distillery on the Virginia Spirits website. Belle Isle produces its flagship Black Label moonshine and four flavored variations: Blood Orange, Cold Brew Coffee, Honey Habanero and Ruby Red Grapefruit. It also offers Belle Isle 100 Proof.

There are other Virginia distilleries legally producing moonshine (see the "Distilleries of the Old Dominion" section of this book for more information). And there are still illegal operations too. Some of the 'shine

A funny postcard of the 1960s showing the hillbilly set making moonshine. Note the "XX" on the jugs—that depicted the purity of the spirit. *Author's collection.*

is made to carry on family traditions, and the quality has a reputation that continues to bring customers. Others make rotgut so cheap that the prices beat out even some of the lowest-priced spirits at the liquor store and create their own market.

Oh, and those *X*s you see—often stereotypically—on moonshine jugs? They have a meaning. Especially in days before modern distilling, when you could get a pure batch of alcohol on the first run through the still and every run through the still, spirits often had to be run several times to filter out impurities. The "XXX" mark on a jug is the distiller's mark promoting that the 'shine has been run through the still three times and that the alcohol is pure. An XXX rating often meant 190 proof or higher.

The practice of using ceramic jugs was more common prior to the mid-nineteenth century, when many moonshiners turned to glass, especially with the patenting of the Mason jar in 1858.

Bootleggers, Moonshiners and Rumrunners

The idea of circumventing the law in regards to alcohol production, sale and enjoyment, like many things in Virginia, has a long history. One of the more notable instances was the bout of unruliness in the late 1700s in paying tax on liquor, which hit folks in the mountains particularly hard and came to a head with the Whiskey Rebellion nearby.

And yet, "For the better part of the 1800s, the United States government left distillers alone," said Jaime Joyce in the book *Moonshine*. Tax was collected for a while to pay off debt in association with the War of 1812, but then things moved right back where they were.

Then a federal tax, which included liquor, was instituted by President Abraham Lincoln to finance the Civil War in 1861 that, at the time, only effected Northern states. The rate increased dramatically following the war and was imposed on the whole nation. It was raised from twenty cents per gallon in 1864 to two dollars per gallon by the time 1868 rolled around, noted Joyce. "The steep tax would lead to an outbreak of illicit distilling." Revenue agents began cracking down on illegal trade across Virginia and the nation.

Moonshining—in this case meaning the non-licensed production of a spirit—to this day is equal parts alcohol and intrigue. Regardless of before, during or after Prohibition, moonshiners have one goal: to try to outrun one thing or another, whether federal agents, the police or tax revenuers.

That fact was highlighted in the 1953 folk song "Copper Pot," written by Albert Frank Beddoe and recorded by such greats as Chet Atkins, Joan Baez and Bob Dylan. Some of the lyrics go:

My daddy he made whiskey, my granddaddy he did too,
We ain't paid no whiskey tax since 1792.

Now, at the turn of the twentieth century and with the rumblings of Prohibition off in the distance, a proliferation of moonshining was starting to kick into high gear.

By 1909, most of Virginia and about half of the Blue Ridge were "dry," and legally operating distilleries were forced to close, according to the Blue Ridge Institute & Museum, part of Ferrum College, located in Franklin County. Here, and across the state, the demand of alcohol was being supplied by illegal stills. But here it seemed that something extraordinary was happening.

In Virginia's mountains, the institute noted the shift by showing use of a smaller turnip pot still up until the first decade or two. Moonshiners and bootleggers would set up deep in the woods on a stream with cool running water and buy fruit from local orchards to make apple brandy or grain from local mills to craft corn whiskey. With the advent of a new type of still, the capacity of moonshine production expanded.

"Around World War I, Blue Ridge moonshining saw the rise of the large submarine-type still," noted the institute. "More gallons of whiskey could be made with one still, and the bootlegger could increase his output dramatically. By the time Prohibition ended [1933], moonshining was a dynamic economic force in the southern Virginia mountains, and its vitality did not lag with the reintroduction of legal alcohol sales."

Autos were still mostly rare and many roads were still rural, so wagons made their way into town or perhaps to a railroad stop. The institute continued, "Oral history in Franklin County tells of individuals making day trips by train to Roanoke with suitcases filled with jars of whiskey." But within the first few decades of the 1900s, with cars and trucks becoming more commonplace, the scope of the moonshining expanded.

Moonshining was a major economic generator, according to an article in the June 16, 1919 issue of the *Alexandria Gazette*. "Moonshiners Prosper; Make Whiskey Main Industry in Southwestern Virginia," the headline read. "Making blockade whisky is the principal industry of the southwestern part of Virginia. Almost every man in this section either is or has been a

This circa 1950 postcard depicts a moonshine still operation deep in the woods. Note the large glass jars to be filled. *Author's collection.*

moonshiner. The country is so mountainous and the soil so poor that there is very little farming. Wheat and corn are practically the only crops grown. The wheat makes bread; the corn makes whisky."

In 1935, reporting on what was called the "Great Moonshine Conspiracy Trial," Sherwood Anderson wrote for *Liberty* magazine, "What is the wettest section in the U.S.A., the place where, during prohibition and since, the most illicit liquor has been made? The extreme wet spot, per number of people, isn't in New York or Chicago. By the undisputed evidence given at a recent trial in the United States Court at Roanoke, Virginia, the spot that fairly dripped illicit liquor, and kept right on dripping it after prohibition ended, is in the mountain country of southwestern Virginia—in Franklin County, Virginia."

He had proof to back it up, with evidence showing that in a county with a population of twenty-four thousand at a time, some 70,448 pounds of yeast were imported, as well as a staggering 34 million pounds of sugar. Anderson noted, "There were said to be single families in the county that used 5,000 pounds of sugar a month."

But moonshining wasn't just a mountain industry; it was found across the state, including Coastal Virginia, as indicated in the May 22, 1921 headline of the *Virginian-Pilot and the Norfolk Landmark*: "Swamps of Princess Anne and Norfolk Counties Pour Out Stream of Moonshine." With mergers and consolidations of municipalities in the 1960s, Princess Anne and Norfolk Counties would later be instrumental in forming the current cities of Chesapeake, Norfolk, Portsmouth and Virginia Beach.

"Since prohibition became generally effective something more than a year ago, the business of illicit manufacture of whisky has grown by leaps and bounds in this section of the state as in other sections. So widely known has it become, in fact, that 'Princess Anne Corn' has been developed into a type phrase," the article noted. It also speculated that the region could become the state's moonshine mecca.

The article continued, "It is said that nearly every patch of woods in Norfolk County, provided it is situated with some little degree of privacy, as contained or now boasts of its own moonshine still. It is said, also, that any night a traveler though Norfolk County may see the gleam and twinkling of countless lights in fields and woods and beside the little forest streams which tells the story of a 'moonshine' still, where John Barleycorn is dying hard, and where some citizen is sneering at the law."

"'You can't throw a rock in Norfolk County,' declared Federal Agent [J.J.] Shugart, 'without hitting an expert moonshiner,'" added the article.

Just a few years into the Noble Experiment, Virginia's reputation as a leading moonshining state was being cemented. "The number of distilleries destroyed in the State of Virginia in the month of December far surpassed all previous records," said Samuel R. Brame, a Prohibition supervisor for the Internal Revenue Service, in an article in the January 16, 1920 issue of the *Highland Recorder*—the number was noted as being more than one thousand.

Brame's district oversaw Virginia, Kentucky, North Carolina, South Carolina and Tennessee, with the newspaper saying that "this district is admitted to be by far the worst. More lawlessness exists and greater number of violations of the law are expected to occur in these five states than in all the rest of the United States combined." He advocated more law enforcement: "We are doing our utmost to cope with the situation but the task is a stupendous one." Brame noted that the Anti-Saloon League was campaigning to raise funds to pay for more "dry agents," as they were called.

Supporting Brame's position, accounts of moonshining were frequent throughout Prohibition. In the January 3, 1920 issue of the *Richmond Times-Dispatch*, an article noted, "Virginia moonshiners receive a larger compensation for their efforts than do United States congressmen, according to the Internal Revenue office here after the seizure of an illicit whiskey-making still of five gallons capacity last night, from the operations of which,

Law enforcement officers destroying moonshine stills in Virginia Beach. *Library of Congress.*

they declare, the owner could have made $25 a day clear profit.…The outfit was seized in a shed near Taylor's crossing on the Richmond, Fredericksburg and Potomac Railway in Henrico County."

"Revenue Officers Palmer, Hurt, Davis and Lowry made what is termed the biggest moonshine still raid that Wise county has ever had," read an article in the *Big Stone Gap Post* on March 31, 1920. "They stole into the moonshine district of the mountains unobserved last Friday and Saturday and succeeded in capturing and destroying ten stills, all within two miles of the Pound, Va., post office."

In the August 14, 1921 issue of the *Virginian-Pilot and the Norfolk Landmark*, an example of the corruption that was part of moonshining was featured in an article: "Federal warrant for the arrest of Albert Willis, police officer of Norfolk County, on the charge of operating an illicit distillery, was issued yesterday by United States Commissioner Mahone.…Willis was taken in custody when, in company with Phillip Jones, alias Blair, he approached a still near which the revenue officers had lain in ambush."

It stated that the arrest was part of two weeks of raids of "moonshine factories" in the county, and another still was destroyed just two miles away. The article noted, "The still was found set up in a tent, only about 500 feet from the road, and about the same distance from the house of Willis. It was of 40-gallon capacity, and in the tent with it were about 600 gallons of mash, eleven fermenters, numerous jugs and various other paraphernalia."

Like for all the stills law enforcement raided, they cut them open and rendered them useless, while at the same time busting bottles of the 'shine, letting it flow into the ground. Sometimes larger sites were blown to kingdom come with dynamite. Folks rounded up in the raids were put in jail or sometimes fined.

Clearly, Prohibition had changed the face of moonshine and moonshiners. That was the subject of the *Virginian-Pilot and the Norfolk Landmark* on August 28, 1926, which read: "Along the stately, smoky mountain ranges which run thorough the Western section of Virginia and thrust their unbroken, cloud-tipped beauty into Kentucky or Tennessee, is the home of a legion of tall, soft-spoken, quiet men, slow to anger but terribly quick on the trigger when aroused who have been accustomed since the very beginning of their first generation to manufacture in apparatus of their own devising the product they have affectionately describe as 'moonshine likker.'"

It continued, "'Pro'ibeeshun's done played hell with stillin' around hyar,' is the burden of their complaint.…It isn't the enforcement of prohibition, per se, that has given the old mountain distiller cause for the bulk of his complaint. There have always been the revenue laws to plaque him, but they really didn't plague him much, after all."

The problem, the article concluded, was the overabundance of illicit alcohol flooding the market because of Prohibition—some offered discreetly by mail order and some, albeit lesser quality, at cut-rate prices: "Men who, in other days, knew where to go in the hills and bring back a jub of pure, but powerful corn liquor whenever they felt in need of it, now can have a case of guaranteed genuine rye liquor set down on their front porches, in a most business like fashion, and at only a moderate increase over the pre-Volstead price. This liquor is shipped to them by express from New York, and elsewhere, by very business like gentlemen who take the risk, what there is of it, and seldom get caught. The liquor is shopped at current bootleg prices, plus $10 a case, which is said to be 'protection.'" Of note, *jub* is a variation on the word *jug*, used for a vessel specifically holding spirits.

Traditional moonshiners did not, as the article argued, like the new wave of hooch. "'Sugar likker,' or liquor manufactured from mash which has been sugared to speed up its maturity, has grown so common that many corn liquor drinkers confess that they are disgusted with the whole situation." Many weren't even taking time to grow or harvest corn, much less purchase corn kernels; they bought cornmeal already ground and ready to turn to mash.

Moonshining, bootlegging, all of it, had become big business. It was about turning out a product quickly and in large numbers. Although there were still small operators, it now included the likes of organized crime. Nationally, names like Al Capone, Charles "Lucky" Luciano and Bugsy Siegel were synonymous with moonshining and bootlegging.

Corruption ran rampant, as was the case with the "Great Moonshine Conspiracy Trial" in 1935. Prosecutors argued that a conspiracy ring of bootleggers and associates worked in the production and distribution of illicit alcohol from 1928 to 1935 in and around Franklin County, defrauding the government of some $5.5 million in whiskey excise taxes—almost $1 billion today. Of eighty folks indicted, there were twenty convictions that included law officers and government officials.

Across Virginia and nationwide, law enforcement was often kept at bay with moonshiners paying hush money, known as a "granny fee," although some had bigger stakes in the industry. But regardless of the public face, for many, the moonshiner remained that mountain man character, a folk hero of sorts. "Historically he has been portrayed as a poor man simply trying to make a living, and indeed years ago making bootleg whiskey was arguably the most sensible way for some families to keep food on the table during hard times," noted the Blue Ridge Institute & Museum. "When factories brought jobs to the Blue Ridge and economic circumstances became easier, the bootlegger was still seen as a free man 'beating the system.' The hypocrisy of the Prohibition era, when everyone from politicians to field laborers continued to drink, only added to the moonshiner's image."

Another folk hero emerged from moonshining: liquor haulers. These were folks who modified their "liquor cars" to outrun law enforcement and revenuers. The vehicles on the outside were stock—that is, there wasn't necessarily anything to differentiate their outward appearance from other vehicles. But they were lightened and reinforced and their engines souped up.

When some of the liquor haulers weren't running 'shine, they were participating in a new sport becoming popular in the 1940s that utilized their driving skills: stock car racing, a forerunner to NASCAR. "You had to have fast cars to haul your whiskey to the people and to get away from the revenue and the ABC and the federal officers," said NASCAR's legendary

Hall of Famer Robert Glenn "Junior" Johnson in an interview with the BBC on December 31, 2013. "If it hadn't been for whiskey, NASCAR wouldn't have been formed. That's a fact." Johnson received a full pardon in 1985 from President Ronald Reagan for a 1956 conviction for crafting illegal whiskey that had landed him in a federal penitentiary for eleven months and postponed his NASCAR career.

Moonshine never went away. Even after the repeal of Prohibition, some towns and counties remained dry. Folks still looked for ways to make money and for ways to evade taxes. In the 1960s, many folks were acquainted with moonshine for the first time—on their television set—during the Rural Revolution, where networks shifted toward sitcoms with country settings and/or situations. A little jug marked with "XXX" made more than one appearance on shows such as *The Beverly Hillbillies*, *Green Acres* and *Petticoat Junction*.

Folks still make illicit 'shine; in fact, the 2008 Recession seemed to mark an increase in still production, noted Alcoholic Beverage Control (ABC) agent Chris Goodmen in the *Roanoke Times* in 2010. More interest on the subject was highlighted with Discovery Channel's launch of the television show *Moonshiners* in 2011 and the 2012 motion picture *Lawless*, based on Matt Bondurant's historic novel *The Wettest County in the World*.

Rumrunning was akin to what the liquor haulers were doing, but by sea. It occurred along every stretch of coast in America. In Virginia, rumrunners carried liquor from the Bahamas, Bermuda, Canada and other places where it could be had, sometimes in fleets of boats. The boats would hover off the Virginia coast at least three miles in international waters, waiting for the opportunity to run into port and drop off their load or to have a small craft come and grab a shipment from them. Usually that was at nighttime, when the rumrunners could find some privacy in the countless coves and inlets along the shoreline.

The Coast Guard and Prohibition agents were at the ready, but the rumrunners had their secrets too. Skillful piloting brought cases of illicit alcohol ashore in Norfolk, according to the *Virginian-Pilot and the Norfolk Landmark* on May 20, 1923:

> *Approximately 10,000 cases of contraband liquor have been landed hereabout in the last ten days it was said on high authority last night, while another report indicated that a big steamer, loaded with fully as much contraband, was waiting outside for an opportunity to run the blockade, either up the Chesapeake or the Potomac....According to reports reaching the Coast Guard, the 10,000-case shipment was transferred from the mother*

One of the rumrunners at night and its nemesis, the *K-13091*, alongside the *Seneca* at the end of the chase, circa 1924. *Library of Congress.*

ship at sea to a smaller craft. The small boats, some as fast as automobiles, shot through the capes under cover of darkness and proceeded to some of the hundreds of inlets in the bay.

A dramatic chase was described in the December 21, 1933 issue of the *Virginian-Pilot and the Norfolk Landmark*: "It was on the night of December 10, 1932 that the Coast Guard patrol Boat CG-163 was cruising in the waters of Chesapeake Bay near Old Plantation Light when she sighted the Matilda Barry running without lights. A flare was sent into the mist to warn the rum runner the Coast Guard boat was near and a signal was given for her to stop."

Making evasive maneuvers, the captain fell overboard and drowned. "Coast Guardsmen swarmed aboard and arrested three men and seized 419 cases of choice foreign liquors." A year after the incident, the newspaper noted, a federal judge forfeited ownership of the boat to the Coast Guard.

Much like with moonshining, rumrunning often had elements of organized crime. A May 26, 1923 article in the *Virginian-Pilot and the Norfolk*

Landmark described the business of William L. Burwell, also known as William E. Baker, who was arrested with his wife and another accomplice in the Atlantic Hotel in Norfolk on charges of unlawfully conspiring to smuggle and transfer intoxicating liquors into the United States. Burwell described himself as "second in command of the Atlantic Coast rum fleet" and part of "a gigantic smuggling syndicate with important branches in New York, Canada, London, Scotland and the Bermudas." Burwell had been in Norfolk two weeks, authorities told the newspaper, arranging for some five or six thousand cases of imported liquors to be brought ashore from his four British-flagged vessels—the *Istar*, the *Cartona*, the *Strand Hill* and the schooner *Mary Beatrice*—anchored three miles off the mouth of the Chesapeake Bay.

The newspaper gave insight as to how vast the business was:

> The syndicate controlling the rum fleet, the authorities have been informed, is comprised of prominent men in New York City and abroad.... Representatives, known as business agents, according to the Federal authorities, operates in conjunction with the masters of the rum ships from shore, receiving orders from the home office.
>
> Sometimes the business agents accompanied the rum ships across the Atlantic, it is said, and upon arrival in this country reported to the American syndicate members for instructions as to the disposition of cargos.
>
> In many large cities, the authorities were informed, the principal bootleggers frequently pool large sums of money to negotiate a deal with the business representative of the rum ship for an entire cargo.

Although Prohibition ended in 1933, bootlegging, moonshining and rumrunning never went away. In fact, it's still around today. Although some folks make their own spirits or bring them in for personal or small-time use, or as a form of individual expression, the main reason it's done on a large-scale basis is simply money. Doing so helps the folks making the drink avoid paying taxes on their product.

Many folks held the following sentiment, as noted by Sara Quinn Hambrick in her 1993 work, *The Quinn Clan*: "Some people believe that everything in moonshining boils down to the almighty dollar and who is going to get it—the government or the moonshiner. Some question which is the greedier of the two."

One of the more noted moonshiners of post-Prohibition times was Amos Law, a Franklin County boy who began his career in peddling white lightning at age sixteen in 1952. By the 1970s, he had become a leader in the illicit business, with a dozen men working under him and distribution along the East Coast. According to his obituary in the *Roanoke Times*, he had a customer base in Baltimore, Philadelphia and New York. He became a Virginia legend.

Law was often in and out of jail and was charged, with others, in Operation Lightning Strike in 1999 by federal authorities, alleging his involvement in the production of more than 481,000 gallons of untaxed liquor from 1992 to 1999. He was acquitted.

Law died at his home in Rocky Mount at age eighty-three in 2019. His son, Henry Law, has written a book about his father and the moonshine industry, *100 Proof*, available on the Law's Choice website. He's also created a legal spirit, Uncle Nearest 1884 Small Batch Whiskey, sold at select ABC stores across Virginia and on the ABC website.

There are other legal moonshines offered across the state today—and if you know the right person, plenty of illegal hooch too.

Prohibition: The Noble Experiment

Virginians were a drinking lot—from beer to spirits like rum and whiskey to wine—during much of the colony's first three hundred years. By the time Virginia's 300th birthday rolled around and was celebrated at the Jamestown Exposition in 1907, it was pretty firmly established that Virginians were the sort of folks who like their drink.

But the temperance movement was on the move, and soon, the unthinkable was happening. In 1916, on the cusp of Prohibition, the *Virginian-Pilot* acknowledged, "Virginia…had been a friend to liquor since John Smith and his followers established the first permanent settlement at Jamestown Island in 1607."

Over the years, there were occasional laws to curb public drunkenness and also pushes for temperance, some beginning in the late eighteenth century as alcohol production proliferated and booze was cheaper. Folks noted an increase in alcoholism and the social issues that follow it. By 1800, a temperance association had formed in Virginia; it formally railed against the production and sale of intoxicating beverages. Toward the end of the nineteenth century, the movement had a stronghold in Virginia and across the nation.

In 1901, the Virginia Anti-Saloon League was founded at a meeting in Richmond, and the June 7, 1902 *Virginian-Pilot* reported, "The Anti-Saloon

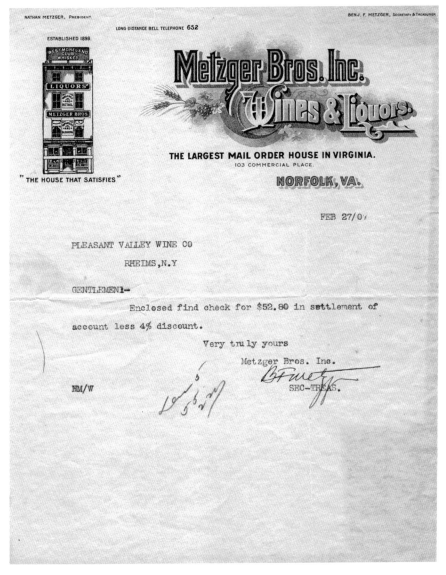

A billhead of Metzger Bros. Inc. Wines & Liquors just a few years prior to Virginia going dry, February 27, 1907. The Norfolk business claimed to be "the largest mail order house in Virginia." *Author's collection.*

League of Virginia is preparing to establish temperance saloons in various portions of the state. They will consist of reading-rooms, parlors and soft-drink counters. Several have already been established, and there has been a decrease in drunkenness in those localities."

Left: Cartoon from the front page of the *Virginian-Pilot* newspaper on the eve of Virginia turning dry, October 31, 1916, depicting a bar scene. "Just in time." *Author's collection.*

Right: Cartoon from the front page of the *Virginian-Pilot* newspaper on the eve of Virginia turning dry, October 31, 1916, depicting a bar scene. "Stowing away the last one and taking home a deckload." *Author's collection.*

Four years before the national ban on alcohol sales, Virginia went dry on November 1, 1916, with the Mapp Law, thanks to the efforts of the Woman's Christian Temperance Union and the Anti-Saloon League. Laws like the 1903 Mapp Law and 1908 Byrd Law set many industry-killing restrictions in place.

This affected a wide group of Virginians—most bar and saloon owners, brewers, distillers and winemakers were forced out of business if they were not able to adapt to another line of business. It also affected restaurant owners, who had to forfeit alcohol on their menus. The Mapp Law was strict, defining "ardent spirits" as "alcohol, brandy, whiskey, rum, gin, wine, porter, ale, beer, all malt liquors, absinthe, and all compounds or mixtures of any of them."

On the last legal day of alcohol possession in Virginia—October 31, 1916—the *Virginian-Pilot* noted, "At midnight tonight the guillotine will fall upon the head of Old Man John B. Tanglefoot, a resident of Virginia since 1607....[T]he boisterous revelry in some of Norfolk's clubs and saloons will be in marked contrast with joyous thanksgiving in many homes and in the churches."

Because of the anticipated antics as folks had one—or more—last legal drinks, Norfolk's mayor issued orders not allowing certain Halloween activities in areas where bars were concentrated "on Main, Granby, or Church streets." But the paper also reported that some saloons were already closed, "depleted of their stocks" in a run by customers leading up to the final date. It noted that in Portsmouth, "[o]ne of the bars at County and Crawford streets was dark last night save for a tiny electric globe that cast its faint rays over a desolate scene of empty shelves, abandoned glasses, and general disorder."

"Ready for Hallowe'en to Go 'Dry' Tonight," read the headline of the October 31, 1916 *Alexandria Gazette*. "When Father Time strikes the hour of twelve tonight he will also ring out the business Alexandria's 39 places of business in which liquors are sold and a total number of 650 throughout the state....Tomorrow will be the first time since the days of the civil war that this city has not had saloons. Some of them closed their doors for the last time on Saturday night but most of them will remain open until 12 o'clock tonight."

On the last day before Prohibition, folks made one last effort to stock up at home, noted the *Alexandria Gazette* on October 31, 1916:

> *With but a few hours left in which intoxicating beverages may be sold legally in Virginia, reports from all parts of the State tell of vast quantities of the liquor being stored away in the homes of citizens for further use.*
>
> *In Richmond today hundreds of moving vans and delivery wagons have formed an almost endless procession, and thousands of gallons have been delivered to private homes. The right of citizens to keep more than the amount stipulated in the new prohibition law remains to be tested in the courts. Every city and town in the State tells the same story of liquor being stored away in large quantities.*

But they'd better keep their drinking at home. The October 31, 1916 issue of the *Richmond Times-Dispatch* noted that even "simple drunks" were going to feel the effects of Prohibition. "Announcement by the Chief of Police that after November 1, even 'simple drunks' must be taken to Police Court indicates a determination to enforce the spirit as well as the letter of the prohibition laws. Heretofore, in order to save unnecessary expenses, it has been the custom of the Police Department to keep simple drunks in the station houses until sobered and then to discharge them."

None of it stopped anyone from getting a drink who wanted a drink. Parts of Virginia bordered other states that had yet to go dry, such as

Maryland. The October 31, 1916 *Alexandria Gazette* reported, "The fact that Alexandria is a border town leads people here to the conclusion that the state commissioner will watch it very carefully, to see that the law is complied."

The alternative was to drink nothing at all, except perhaps one of the many soft drinks that proliferated during this time. Indeed, bubbly, carbonated, sugary drinks have one part of their story firmly in the role as temperance drinks or alternatives to alcoholic beverages, dating back to the nineteenth century. In fact, a Coca-Cola advertisement on the front page of the May 27, 1887 *Virginian-Pilot read*: "Coca Cola! The Pleasant Exhilarant. Refreshing and Invigorating Popular Soda Fountain Drink containing the tonic properties of the famous Kolanuts, and Pemberton's French Wine Coca Which destroys the taste for alcoholic stimulants." Note the last line.

Around the time Virginia enacted Prohibition, Norfolk's Gin-Gera, a ginger ale–type drink bottled in the city beginning in 1912, had grown in popularity so much that by 1914 it had expanded into a ten-thousand-square-foot facility on north Granby Street. Close by at the corner of Church and Twenty-Sixth Streets, Lemon-Kola, producer of a lemon-lime beverage, opened a distribution center in 1916.

Also in 1916, Nisco cola came onto the scene from the Consolidated Bottling Works in downtown Norfolk. The unusual name came as the result of a contest; Hunter Price of Norfolk and R. Howard of Newsoms won twenty dollars in gold as the first prize for selecting the moniker. Other Virginia cities also had an increase in soft drink popularity, whether local, regional or national brands picked up at a store or enjoyed at a lunch counter or soda fountain.

Then, on January 17, 1920, the whole nation went dry with the enactment of the Eighteenth Amendment to the U.S. Constitution, which prohibited the manufacture, sale or transportation of intoxicating liquors in the United States. "Dry's Dream Comes True After Fight for Years," was a headline of the *Richmond Times-Dispatch* on January 17, 1920. "Nation-Wide Prohibition Effective at Last by Decision of Forty-Six Sovereign States." A *Virginian-Pilot* headline on the same day put it more directly: "Nationwide Ban Placed on Booze Now Effective."

The Volstead Act, also known as the National Prohibition Act, expanded the scope of the Eighteenth Amendment and already-enacted War Prohibition Act later in the year. This specified what the strength of alcohol that was prohibited could be, what the penalties for breaking the law were and the

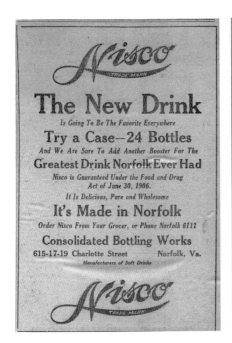

Left: Nisco was a soft drink bottled in Norfolk, circa 1910. Many new soft drinks were introduced during this era as an alternative to alcoholic beverages. *Author's collection.*

Right: An October 1918 advertisement for Apple-O, "a pippin of a drink" promising a champagne sparkle and a champagne flavor. Crafted in Norfolk, this is one of the soft drinks made by businesses to supplement the loss of alcohol sales due to Prohibition. *Author's collection.*

exceptions that could be made in the law for medicinal or religious regions or for scientific research.

Interestingly, the law did not prohibit folks from *drinking* alcoholic beverages, but it made it nearly impossible to legally get them. And yet, alcohol flowed. In homes and in the back of businesses, speakeasies popped up, serving spirits on the sly. Many roads in Virginia were rural, and much of the coastline in the eastern part of the state was desolate, making transportation, especially at night, difficult for authorities trying to prevent smuggling.

Some folks turned to making small batches of alcohol in their homes, and others had larger-scale operations. Some turned to moonshine. "Moonshine in Virginia was hitting its peak [during Prohibition]," noted the Virginia Spirits website. Moonshine operations increased. Smugglers brought in contraband from the sea. Folks had doctors write prescriptions for whiskey for various ailments.

Above: Policeman standing alongside a wrecked car following a chase and cases of confiscated moonshine, November 16, 1922. *Library of Congress.*

Right: A woman discreetly slipping a flask of illicit spirits into her Russian boot in a Washington, D.C., establishment on January 21, 1922. *Library of Congress.*

The Bureau of Prohibition was created as a federal mandate to stop alcohol sales, and agents patrolled in cars with insignia plates like this to uphold the law. *Library of Congress.*

In stills in the marshes and swamps of Coastal Virginia, in deeply wooded areas through the Piedmont and Northern Virginia, as well as in the hollers and valleys of the mountains, more moonshine was being made. By 1935, Franklin County was noted as the "Moonshine Capital of the World," producing more of the spirit than anywhere else in the country.

During the seventeen years that Prohibition had its death grip on Virginia, there was some slang that was developed that was the cat's pajamas:

"barrel house": a distribution place for illicit alcohol; also "gin mill."

"bee's knees": something really cool, swell. Other names: "cat's meow," "cat's pajamas," "eel's hips" or "snake's hips."

"bent": drunk. Other names: "blotto," "boiled as an owl," "canned," "fried," "plastered," "spifflicated" and "zozzled."

"blind tiger" or "blind pig": a place where illicit alcohol is sold.

"booze cruise": a short boat ride into non-U.S. territorial waters, such as the Atlantic Ocean, for the purpose of drinking alcohol where the government has no jurisdiction.

"bubbles": champagne.

"bull": policeman; also "fuzz," reportedly because officers would write up many small violations and be fussy over minor incidents.

"butter and egg man": a man who rolls into town with a lot of cash looking for a good time and ready to spend it in speakeasies, inferring it is a farmer who recently came into money and is visiting the city.

"cellar smeller": someone who comes around when free alcohol is served.

"coffin varnish": alcohol; also "giggle water," "hooch," "horse liniment," "panther sweat," "stuff" and "tarantula juice." Most are references to inferior-quality spirits.

"dead soldier": an empty glass that had previously held an alcoholic beverage.

"dewdropper": a lazy young man who sleeps during the day and hangs out at juice joints at night.

"dip the bill": have a drink.

"dry": a person in support of Prohibition.

"dry agent": someone employed as an officer of the Bureau of Prohibition.

"86'd": bounced from a bar or club. In Jef Klein's book *The History and Stories of the Best Bars of New York*, he claimed that during Prohibition police on the take would give Chumley's Bar at 86 Bedford Street in the West Village of Lower Manhattan short notice of a raid. The bar would quickly push patrons out onto 86th Street as police raided the other entrance on Pamela Court.

"flapper": a free-spirited woman who dressed up and liked to spend a night on the town, often in speakeasies or illicitly run bars or clubs.

"foot juice": cut-rate, cheap wine.

"hair of the dog": a hangover cure, consisting of a shot of additional alcohol.

"jazz": something exciting; also "jazzed," "jazzed up" and "jazzy."

"juice joint": an illicit bar or club; another name for a speakeasy or nip joint.

"needle beer": non-alcoholic beer spiked with alcohol by using a needle to inject the spirit through the corks of a bottle or keg.

"real McCoy": high-quality alcohol.

"rotgut": grossly inferior-quality alcohol.

"snake charmer": a female bootlegger.

"wet": the opposite of dry; a person opposed to Prohibition.

"whale": a heavy drinker.

During Prohibition's thirteen-year run, the U.S. Treasury allowed licensed physicians to write their patients a prescription for spirits, to be taken in regular intervals, much like any other medicine. These were dosed out for a number of reasons, among them depression and indigestion. Scribbled on government-issued prescription pads, the doctors would fill out basic information like patient name, the kind of liquor to be offered and the quantity.

According to *Smithsonian Magazine*, the doctor might specify whiskey or another spirit, and the pharmacist might fill the order with a cheaper brand or a premium brand. A dose was usually an ounce every few hours, and a patient typically left with a pint of spirits to last ten days.

The article noted that the doctor also charged about three dollars for writing the prescription, and it cost another three to four dollars for having the prescription filled. Three dollars in 1922 is roughly equivalent to forty-five dollars in 2021.

WALK SOFTLY AND CARRY A. NATION

One of the nation's more interesting footnotes in regards to the temperance movement that lead to Prohibition was Carrie (sometimes spelled Carry) Amelia Nation. Despite her reputation, which seemed to be one part evangelist and one part huckster, with a dash of psycho thrown in, her relentlessness worked on getting press (remember, even bad press is good press) for the argument of a country going dry.

The Kentucky-born Nation, whose first husband died an alcoholic, began her crusade against spirits (and later tobacco and other vices) in Kansas in 1900. She preached sermons and often took up rocks and a signature hatchet to break up saloons across the country, including in Virginia. Here, at the Onyx Bar in Norfolk around the turn of the twentieth century, she threw the axe and shattered the mirror in the opulent bar. These actions she would later call "hatchetations."

During her time in the limelight, she crisscrossed the Old Dominion. At her stops in Virginia and elsewhere, she peddled booklets and miniature hatchets as souvenirs to pay for her expenses. "Carrie Nation, the temperance agitator, who will deliver two addresses in [Roanoke], made a crusade on the saloons yesterday," wrote the *Newport News Daily Press* on December 29, 1906. "She first went to one of the most fashionable resorts in the city where a crowd of about one hundred soon gathered. She used no hatchet, but her tongue was freely used....She went from saloon to saloon, where she spoke to the proprietors and customers. At one place she was ejected and the door locked in her face. She then spoke to the crowd assembled on the street."

Nation ventured to Norfolk a few days later on January 10, 1907, with the idea of preaching her gospel and seeking out opportunities to showcase her message at the upcoming Jamestown Exposition. The Jamestown Expo was a world's fair–type celebration of the 300th anniversary of the settlement of Jamestown. It was held, with much fanfare, in Norfolk from April 26 until December 1, 1907, and included military operations, exhibitions, a midway and more. President Theodore Roosevelt was in attendance, as were many other notables, such as the humorist Samuel L. Clemens, better known as Mark Twain, and luminary and scholar Booker T. Washington. Carrie Nation wanted in on the act.

The *Virginian-Pilot* reported on January 9, 1907, that she would be arriving in town the next day, according to her agent, James H. Loh. "She will probably arrange for the YMCA in which to lecture," Loh told the newspaper. But the YMCA had a different idea. The *Virginian-Pilot* reported, "Asked if he knew anything of the proposed visit to the YMCA, Secretary Clements said: 'I have heard nothing of her coming. I doubt seriously whether such a character would be allowed in the YMCA hall.'"

She came anyway but didn't stay long. Her visit to Norfolk was covered in the January 10, 1907 issue of the *Newport News Daily Press* with two simple sentences. Newport News is only separated by water across a harbor: "Carrie Nation is in Norfolk. That is near enough for Newport News people, thank you."

An account of her day in Norfolk was chronicled in the January 10, 1907 *Virginian-Pilot*:

> *Mrs. Nation is a woman of sixty years of age. She wore black, and a black shawl and bonnet were added for her street attire. Her appearance on the streets of Norfolk at first created much amusement, but she soon got many of them "going" with lectures. Young men with cigarettes were stopped and told to throw away the "degraded filth."*
>
> *She tackled James Jones, of buffet fame* [owner of Welcome Restaurant]*, and handed him a warm lecture. Mr. Jones greeted her cordially at first, but when Mrs. Nation began to sling the "King's English" in a continual cataract at him, he quietly moved away.*
>
> *She moved up and down Main, Granby and Church streets all through the day, but did not enter a saloon, although it is said she had planned a raid.*
>
> *When she first arrived in Norfolk, she followed the crowd and landed in the* [Jamestown] *Exposition headquarters. There she met Chief Sutton of the Press Bureau, and told him she didn't like expositions because they made too much noise. She afterward supplemented her remark by declaring that she wanted a monopoly on the noise-making.*

Then she started on her hunt for a hall, and met with disappointment everywhere, she declaring the YMCA and other organizations had all turned her down.

When seen by a Virginian-Pilot reporter, Mrs. Nation talked freely of her crusades. She reiterated her much-repeated sermon on tobacco and whisky, declaring they were "tools of the devil." Four newspaper reporters approached Mrs. Nation at one time, and all "unthinkingly" were smoking cigarettes, except one, and that one was told he need only deny he had not because she "could smell the vile odor on him."

In speaking of the Jamestown Exposition, Mrs. Nation declared she disapproved of them, because they were as a rule backed and supported by the brewing interests.

"All I hear about Jamestown Exposition is of the beer shops it will contain," she said. Speaking of Norfolk, she said its reputation abroad as a "vile, bad town" was too well established for her to take time to discuss it.

After a long tirade against whisky, tobacco, bad women, bad men, and the entire category of evil, Mrs. Nation branched off on politics and the next presidential candidates.

Nation found no place welcoming her and no one assisting her in Norfolk that day, and she decided to leave.

The January 10, 1907 *Newport News Daily Press* wrote, "Mrs. Nation sought the Woman's Christian Temperance Union, but they declined to aid her in an effort to get a hall to speak here. Failing on every hand to get a hall she returned tonight to Washington, from where she came this morning."

But within a month, the February 12, 1907 headlines of the *Virginian-Pilot* read, "Carrie Nation to Be Attraction at [Jamestown] Expo." In the article, her agent, James Loh, who set up a Norfolk office, said that she would raise a "huge tent—a tabernacle…just outside the grounds where she will preach temperance.…Of course, she's going to be the star attraction." The article noted that Loh invited the reporter "down to Jimmy Jones' and let's have a drink" to talk more. This is the same James Jones of Welcome Restaurant whom Nation had belittled on the streets of Norfolk during her ill-fated January visit.

The April 26 opening date of the Jamestown Exposition came and went, and the fair ran for the next eight months. There is no article or advertisement of Carrie Nation or her tented tabernacle as part of the event during any of the expo's run—except one: at the Miller Brothers' 101 Ranch Show, which was by all accounts a spectacular extravaganza of cowboys, cowgirls, Native

Americans, horses, steers and more. The show also included buffaloes, including one named Carrie Nation.

The fiery prohibitionist died at age sixty-four in 1911, not living long enough to see her dream of a national Prohibition, which would come eight years following her passing—nor what would surely have been a nightmare for her with the rebuke and repeal of Prohibition thirteen years after it became the law of the land.

Repeal and the Alcohol Beverage Control

"What America needs now is a drink," said President Franklin Roosevelt, echoing the sentiments of many as the Eighteenth Amendment establishing Prohibition was repealed on December 5, 1933, by the Twenty-First Amendment. It is the only Constitutional amendment to be repealed in its entirety.

Virginia voted by a 63 percent margin for repeal, but a legacy of Prohibition still remains in Virginia today: the Department of Alcoholic Beverage Control (ABC), established on March 7, 1934. This state agency regulates all aspects of alcohol sales in the state, even running all the retail liquor stores across Virginia, although beer and wine can be sold in shops such as convenience stores and supermarkets. The regulation of liquor sales extends to Virginia's restaurants too: spirits must be purchased through the ABC. The agency also restricts the amount of alcohol a restaurant can serve based on a formula of how much its overall sales include food and regulates the wording in certain advertisements. Until the late 2000s, simple phrases like "Happy Hour" to describe drink specials were forbidden. Until 1968, Virginia restaurants were prohibited from selling drinks, and for a time after that, customers couldn't stand or walk while holding an alcoholic beverage.

The Chesapeake & Ohio (C&O) Railway applied for the first license to serve in October 1968. Fifty-two years since the last drink by the glass was poured, waiter Wilfred Wilson Sr. did the honors on C&O's Food-Bar Car No. 1610, according to the *Richmond Times-Dispatch*, parked at the railroad's Newport News station and later bound for Charlottesville. The *Times-Dispatch* reported, "While waiting for the first official customer, the very first drink was actually made for the reporter covering the big event at 11:08am. The first official legal drink was sold at 1:28pm on Thursday, October 17 to T.P. Skeeter, a 61-year-old operator of a water taxi, whose boat was moored

Above: Bars sprang up in downtown Norfolk following the repeal of Prohibition, offering many vices for sailors and other folks until 1961. *Isabella and Carrol Walker Photograph Collection, Sargeant Memorial Collection, Norfolk Public Library.*

Opposite: Interior of an East Main Street watering hole, downtown Norfolk, circa 1945. *Author's collection.*

near the Newport News station. He had a scotch whisky and soda, which cost $1.14, with $.04 of it being state sales tax."

Bars and restaurants across the Commonwealth also applied for licenses from the Virginia ABC. Drinks again were flowing in public spaces in Virginia, but with restrictions. With ideals established during the temperance movement in mind, a ratio law was established saying that a restaurant had to make at least 45 percent of its income from food sales in order to have a liquor license. Some bars danced around the rule by adding discount bar menus and putting out buffets. Others went with the flow.

An establishment could not obtain a state liquor license from the Virginia ABC in order to serve from a bar; drinks were only served to people seated at a table. The restaurant also had to have more than fifty seats, disadvantaging small operations, and also had to have the right patrons. Legislation read, in part, that an establishment would be shut down if guests exhibited "immoral, indecent, or profane language."

The right kind of employees was a must too, with the edict declaring that the establishment will not "Knowingly employ in the licensed business any person who has the general reputation as a prostitute, homosexual, panderer, gambler, habitual law violator, person of ill repute, user of or peddler of narcotics or person who drinks to excess or any 'B-Girl.'" Don't have any

Matchbook for Kane's Tavern in downtown Norfolk, circa 1945, proclaiming "Drop in for a friendly glass." This was one of the bars and taverns that drew bawdy crowds. *Author's collection.*

investors in your business—the law would not "allow any person to receive a percentage of the income of the licensed business or have any beneficial interest in such business."

Over time, the majority of these regulations have been discarded, with the ratio of alcohol-to-food clause staying in place, although the percentage has been relaxed.

But not every municipality allowed drinking at all. Following repeal, some areas of the state remained dry, although that number has decreased over the decades. As of 2021, the Virginia ABC reports that nine Virginia counties do not permit alcohol sales, or have limited permitting, although beer and wine may be served. In some locations, "Referendums may allow for mixed beverages in certain towns (and supervisor's election districts) located with dry counties." The nine dry counties are Bland, Buchanan, Charlotte, Craig, Grayson, Highland, Lee, Patrick and Russell. Many of these restrictions were, and are, forms of blue laws, which enact a governing body's ideals of morality for the whole.

Perhaps the biggest change in the way Virginians drink since 1968 came in 2020 due to the COVID-19 pandemic. ABC stores began allowing curb pickup at most of its locations the same day the order was placed.

A pilot program was also established to allow shipping "wine, spirits, and mixers to customers' home, reinforcing its commitment to social distancing," noted the agency's 2020 annual report. Another game-changer: Virginia distilleries could ship directly to consumer's homes, and restaurants could provide to-go cocktails in sealed containers for guests. These changes are still in effect as of mid-2021.

POST-PROHIBITION DRINKING

Immediately following repeal, America had to catch up with its liquor production. In Virginia, that began with A. Smith Bowman. Bowman established the 7,200-acre Sunset Hills farm in Fairfax County in 1927 to

Corn was the grain of choice for distilled spirits in Virginia in 1620 and apparently around 1950, when this Indian Queen whiskey was being made in Richmond. *Author's collection.*

operate a dairy and granary. The rich fields yield a lot of grain, and Bowman needed a use for the excess. The answer came in 1934 when he built a distillery on the farmland and crafted Virginia Gentleman; until the 1950s, A. Smith Bowman Distillery was the only legal producer of spirits in Virginia. The distillery relocated to Fredericksburg in 1988 and has received many accolades, including "World's Best Bourbon" at the World Whiskies Award.

Of course Virginians could only drink Bowman's bourbon, and other spirits, by the glass at home, since liquor by the drink wouldn't be established in Virginia until 1968. Some possessed better bartending skills than others, but there wasn't much inspiration—at least, until the end of World War II. With hundreds of thousands of troops returning from theaters in Europe and the Pacific, America's taste buds were about to be shaken—and stirred.

In an interview on Michigan Radio in 2014, Chris Cook, chief restaurant and wine critic at *Hour Detroit Magazine*, explained. The radio report noted, "After the war, Cook says Americans' palates changed, with many young soldiers returning home from deployment after being exposed to food from around the world. Soldiers' families were also privy to more travel due to a boom in disposable income in post-war America."

The same holds true for drinking. One of the first influences popped up with the advent of the Tiki culture. Although origins began in 1933 with Don's Beachcomber, a Polynesian-themed bar and restaurant in Hollywood, California, things exploded in the 1940s and '50s. This was fueled by returning service members who had been in the Pacific and experienced Tiki culture firsthand. They brought home souvenirs of faraway lands and tales of exotic eats and drinks. When the 1949 Rodgers and Hammerstein musical *South Pacific* hit the stage, even more folks had an appetite for the land where palm trees swayed.

While Virginia did not have a Don's Beachcomber or Trader Vic's, Polynesian-inspired spots opened up in cities large and small across the Commonwealth, such as Blue Hawaii in Norfolk. Many emulated drinks from the original Tiki establishments, but as they say, imitation is the sincerest form of flattery. Suddenly couples in the state could sip a fog cutter cocktail from an enormous, elaborately decorated bowl. Mai tais and zombies became de rigueur. The Tiki culture cocktails waned over time but have made a comeback in the 2000s.

Another influence during this time was the charm and sophistication associated with the Camelot era during the presidency of John F. Kennedy. Many folks wanted to emulate the continental and elaborate dinners hosted by First Lady Jacqueline Kennedy. The first lady had hired French chef Rene Verdon to reflect her vision for the White House. According to History.com, "The Kennedys installed a bar in the State Dining Room, complete with butlers to shake and pour martinis and bourbon." One state dinner, held on the lawn at Mount Vernon on July 11, 1961, hosted 140 dignitaries in honor of the president of Pakistan. The National Symphony played as VIPs clinked glasses and dined on French cuisine. Suddenly, cocktail hours and entertaining had a new high-water mark in Virginia and across the country.

The '60s also ushered in the Jet Age, when those with wanderlust could fly quickly and in style to locations across the United States and the globe in a fraction of the time it took before. With more folks jet-setting, the world became smaller and influences on eats and drinks greater. Part of this era was traveling in sophistication, when classic and emerging cocktails were served at your seat while flying along at six hundred miles per hour thirty-nine thousand feet above the earth.

This era didn't last. Beginning around 1960 and running into the 1990s was the Dark Ages of Cocktails. Increasingly, the taste of classic cocktails faded, replaced with overly simplistic and overly sweet drinks, favored in the fern bars of the '60s and '70s, clubs filled with yuppies in the '80s and bars crowded with clubbers in the '90s. Quality was sacrificed for speed, maximum booze, showmanship and garish garnishes in many cases—think of the 1988 Tom Cruise movie *Cocktail*.

These were the Harvey Wallbangers, Long Island ice teas and cosmos. Premade, commercial sour mixes were used, as were bottled lemon and lime juices. Cocktails weren't crafted as much as they were assembled. Vodka emerged as a favored spirit, but only as a boozy base for drinks, allowing for the alcohol impact but no real flavor to counteract other ingredients. This gave rise to the faux-martini craze, like apple-tinis and espresso martinis. These made people feel connected to their parents' martini-loving generation without understanding what a delight a well-made, classic martini was.

The real-deal cocktails were pushed aside, relegated to folks old enough to remember them or the curious who may have heard about them from somewhere. Everything is cyclical, though, and just when you thought you'd never have a perfect Manhattan or old fashioned again, dynamics shifted and the stage was set for returning to the basics—with finesse—in the aughts.

RECIPES

APPLE PIE SHINE

Although historically folks have enjoyed moonshine sipping right from the canning jar, others have cut it with fruit juice or other liquids to make it more palatable. A take on this way of enjoying the spirit is by crafting a batch of apple pie moonshine, which many say is like drinking a glass of apple pie—with a lot of booze mixed in. Our Apple Pie Shine is delicious and easy drinking, but watch out—the effects of the alcohol will sneak up on you.

Variations of this drink were further popularized in episodes of the television show *Moonshiners*, shown on Discovery. The series frequently follows Tim Smith, a Virginia moonshiner who now makes legal hooch at Belmont Farm Distillery.

4 cups natural apple juice
4 cups natural apple cider
¾ cups granulated sugar
¼ cups packed brown sugar
2 cinnamon sticks
1 teaspoon apple pie spice
1 ½ cups moonshine

In a large pot over medium-high heat, add apple juice, cider, granulated sugar, brown sugar, cinnamon sticks and apple pie spice. Bring to a low boil, cover pot and reduce heat to medium-low. Simmer for 1 hour. Remove from heat and allow to cool to room temperature.

Remove the cinnamon sticks, add moonshine and stir. Transfer to three pint-sized, sealable jars. Jars can be refrigerated or stored at room temperature. Shake jars well before serving.

Note: Use commercial apple pie spice or make your own blend. Here's how: In a small sealable jar, add 3 teaspoons ground cinnamon, 2 teaspoons ground nutmeg, 1 teaspoon ground cardamom, ½ teaspoon ground allspice and ½ teaspoon ground ginger. Seal jar and shake to mix. Store, sealed, in a cool dark place for 9–12 months. Yields approximately 6 cups.

VIVA LA CUBA LIBRE

The Cuba Libre, which means "Free Cuba" in Spanish, is also known as a rum and coke. The cocktail was crafted around 1900 to celebrate the island nation's independence following the Spanish-American War. The fizzy concoction became popular in Cuba and across the United States; it still enjoys popularity today. The 1940s calypso song "Rum and Coca-Cola," popularizing the notion of a young man seeking out boozy refreshment and local girls on a Trinidad beach, boosted the drink's recognition.

Note: For a more authentic taste, seek out Mexican Coke, which is still sweetened with cane sugar and not high-fructose corn syrup as with Coca-Colas bottled in America.

3 lime wedges
2 ounces white rum
4 ounces cola; traditionally Coca-Cola is used

In a highball glass squeeze 2 lime wedges and toss in. Muddle with a muddler or end of a wooden spoon. Add white rum and fill glass with ice. Fill with cola and stir. Garnish with remaining lime wedge. Yields 1 cocktail.

PRETTY IN PINK LADY

While the origins of this cheery, turn-of-the-twentieth-century drink are not known, tradition says that the name was inspired by a 1911 Broadway musical of the same name. Popular in speakeasies during Prohibition, its reputation as perhaps the first "girly drink" was established after repeal in the 1930s, when it was shown in women's magazines and other periodicals of the period.

During the 1940s and '50s, it saw a resurgence when movie star and sex symbol Jayne Mansfield commented that she liked to have a pink lady before her meals. The drink again became popular in the 1970s.

Note: The egg white is instrumental in providing the signature froth on top of the drink; use reconstituted powdered egg whites if you have health concerns. For the applejack, we prefer Laird's Applejack, noted for being crafted from Virginia apples since 1780.

1 ½ ounces gin
¾ ounce applejack or apple brandy
¼ ounce fresh-squeezed lemon juice
¼ ounce grenadine
1 egg white
maraschino cherries

In a cocktail shaker, add the gin, applejack, lemon juice, grenadine and egg white and shake vigorously for about 30 seconds. Check to make sure the egg white has fully incorporated into the liquid; if not, shake again. Fill the shaker with ice and shake vigorously for about 30 seconds more and strain into a coupe or martini glass. Pierce three maraschino cherries on a skewer and garnish glass. Yields 1 cocktail.

BLUE HAWAII

One of the classic Tiki drinks found in any Polynesian restaurant worth its weight in leis is the Blue Hawaii. First crafted in 1957 in Hawaii by bartender Harry Yee, the cocktail stirs the sentiments of the tropics not only through its flavors but also through its Pacific blue hue. Have a few of these, and you will be up on a table singing out your best Elvis impersonation. Thank ya, thank ya very much.

¾ ounce vodka
¾ ounce white rum

½ *ounce blue Curaçao*
1 ounce fresh-squeezed lemon juice
pineapple wedge

In a cocktail shaker filled with ice, add vodka, rum, blue Curaçao and lemon juice and shake vigorously. Strain into a tall glass or hurricane glass filled with crushed ice. Garnish with a pineapple wedge and maybe one of those little cocktail umbrellas. Yields 1 cocktail.

A MID-CENTURY MODERN—ISH MARTINI

The martini's origins date back to the late 1800s; indeed, Jerry Thomas's 1887 *Bartender's Guide* lists a drink called the Martinez. Historically, the name is derived from the San Francisco Bay area town of Martinez, where the drink was either crafted there or at the Occidental Hotel in San Francisco, depending on which story you favor. Regardless, the mix, which included more (sweet) vermouth than gin, as well as maraschino liqueur and bitters, wouldn't be the martini we think of today.

Rather, the cocktail evolved over time. By the early 1920s, the ratio of gin to vermouth had shifted, and the common garnishes of an olive or lemon twist were coming onto the scene, although orange or other aromatic bitters were also often used.

During Prohibition, gin was plentiful, and the martini was a popular drink behind the closed doors of speakeasies. Vermouth shifted from sweet to dry, and the ratio shifted too—to 3 parts gin to 1 part vermouth. And because gin was plentiful in the early 1930s following repeal, since whiskey took some time to age, the drink remained so.

By the *Mad Men* days of the 1950s and '60s, the amount of vermouth had been reduced even more, and tastes shifted to the "drier" drink. Most folks think of a dry martini as the standard, which became 15 parts gin to 1 part vermouth.

Along with more leisure time following World War II, a new era of prosperity and the influence of Kennedy's Camelot and the Jet Age, the martini was in its heyday. The "three-martini lunch" was also popularized at this time, noting extravagant lunches often taken by businessmen of the time wheeling and dealing over drinks.

The 1970s saw the popularization of vodka, and many bartenders began shaking and stirring their martinis with that spirit rather than gin. Whimsical drinks like the apple-tini, which are vodka-based, also appeared at this time, with nothing in common with a traditional martini other than the glass used.

But there are variations, including:

- 50/50 martini: a cocktail with equal parts gin and vermouth
- dirty martini: a martini with the addition of a splash of olive brine or olive juice and traditionally garnished with olives
- perfect martini: equal parts sweet and dry vermouth in the drink; this does not change the gin-to-vermouth ratio
- upside-down martini: also called a reverse martini, this drink uses more vermouth than gin
- wet martini: this drink uses more vermouth than the standard ratio but does not reach 50 percent of the beverage

By the 2000s, with the resurgence of many classic cocktails, the martini had once again found a new audience.

Although martinis are usually strained into a glass, they can be served on the rocks. Martinis are also great for making into a large batch for gatherings rather than having to craft each drink individually.

Of note, we like to place our martini glasses in the freezer for about an hour before preparing the drink. We also prefer lemon peel to olives as a garnish because we find the citrus plays better with the botanicals in the gin. We are also firm believers that a classic martini should be stirred and not shaken. Sorry, James Bond.

½ ounce dry vermouth
3 ounces gin
lemon peel or olives

Pour vermouth in a martini glass and swirl glass. Make sure vermouth coats entire glass interior. Discard remaining vermouth. Fill a small glass pitcher with ice and pour in gin. With a metal spoon, stir in a clockwise motion one hundred times. Strain chilled gin into prepared martini glass and garnish with lemon peel or olives. Yields 1 cocktail.

LONG ISLAND ICED TEA

The classic Long Island iced tea, which epitomizes indulgence, has origins in the Me Decade of the 1970s. Tradition says it was first crafted in 1972 during a cocktail competition on Long Island, New York. Five types of spirits, lemon juice or a sour mix and a splash of cola create a drink that looks like iced tea, is smooth drinking and will knock you on your keister. Although there has been a resurgence in popularity periodically from the 1980s through today, the Long Island iced tea is a prime example of the Dark Ages of Cocktails.

½ ounce vodka
½ ounce gin
½ ounce white rum
½ ounce blanco tequila
½ ounce colorless orange liqueur, such as Triple Sec
1 tablespoon fresh-squeezed lemon juice
cola
lemon wedges

In a cocktail shaker filled with ice, add vodka, gin, rum, tequila, orange liqueur and lemon juice. Shake vigorously and pour, including ice, into a tall glass. Top with cola, stir and garnish with lemon wedges. Yields 1 cocktail.

SEX ON VIRGINIA BEACH

Shots, or shooters, saw their popularity explode in the 1970s. As the name implies, these miniature cocktails are served in shot glasses and meant to be thrown back in one big gulp, sometimes with a full-sized drink as an accompaniment. Some shots are as simple as one pour of a single spirit, while others are more complicated and have multiple ingredients. Some are even layered, offering a treat for the eyes as well as the palate.

Some popular shooters of the era included the B-52, Kamikaze and Sex on the Beach. Here's our version of the latter. Note that exact measurements are not given, as shot glass sizes vary; pour accordingly.

I part vodka
I part peach schnapps or peach brandy
I part cranberry juice
I part pineapple juice

Put in shaker with ice and strain into shot glasses.

CANDY APPLE-TINI

While the cosmopolitan was first crafted in the 1930s, the idea of sweet, usually vodka-based cocktails served in a martini glass really took off in 1972 when *Playboy* magazine showcased the Adam's apple martini, later simply known as the apple-tini.

These drinks have nothing in common with a classic martini; for one, vodka is the base instead of gin. The use of vodka in drinks significantly increased in this period because of the ready availability, lack of color and neutral flavor; it's one reason bartenders often call this the Dark Ages of Cocktails.

Rather, they derive their name from being crafted in a cocktail shaker and strained into a martini glass. In the 1980s and '90s, these types of drinks exploded, with popular variations including dessert drinks like the espresso-tini and chocolate-tini. Here's our nod to the 'tini craze.

Glass Rim Ingredients
2 tablespoons turbinado sugar
I teaspoon apple pie spice
lemon wedge

In a shallow bowl add sugar and spice and, with a spoon, stir to mix. Run a lemon wedge around the edge of a martini glass and roll the edge of the glass in the sugar/spice mixture to coat. Allow to sit about 5 minutes before crafting the cocktail.

Cocktail Ingredients
6 ounces natural apple cider
I ½ ounces cinnamon whiskey or cinnamon schnapps
I ½ ounces vodka

dash real vanilla extract
dash apple pie spice
apple wedge
cinnamon stick

In a cocktail shaker, add cider, whiskey, vodka, vanilla and spice. Fill with ice, cover and shake vigorously. Strain into the martini glass. Garnish with an apple wedge and a cinnamon stick.

Note: Use commercial apple pie spice or make your own blend. Here's how: In a small sealable jar add 3 teaspoons ground cinnamon, 2 teaspoons ground nutmeg, 1 teaspoon ground cardamom, ½ teaspoon ground allspice and ½ teaspoon ground ginger. Seal jar and shake to mix. Store, sealed, in a cool dark place for 9–12 months. Yields 1 cocktail.

Chapter 5

THE TWENTY-FIRST CENTURY

Saved by Zero

America entered the twenty-first century on a high note. Folks were excited to reach the year 2000, and they partied like it was 1999—because it was. But almost two years into the aughts, a national disaster with long-lasting effects happened: the September 11 terrorist attacks. It was more than just a destruction of aircraft and buildings (including the Pentagon, on Virginia soil) and loss of some three thousand lives—it was an attempt to destroy the American way of life.

Almost immediately, patriotic flags and other national symbols of all shapes and sizes popped up on places of business and worship, on homes and in yards and flying from car antennae. But something else happened too. It appears that folks began questioning what it was to be an American. From that train of thought, many were pondering what they were already on the cusp of losing, even before the terrorist acts.

We were living in a fast-paced world, and along the way, simple things were being sacrificed. Like sitting down to Sunday suppers like mothers made, where families lingered around the dinner table as the golden hour approached. Shopping at local markets for produce at farms and farm stands on the outskirts of town. Picking up baked goods made that morning in little shops on Main Street, rather than ones from a big-box store that had been mass-produced halfway across the country. Supporting American crafted beer, spirits and wine. The September 11 terrorist attacks seems to have set in motion a revolution of sorts that was already brewing: buy local, support local.

After the mid-twentieth century or so, many dynamics in the world changed. The mass production of goods became the norm, often sacrificing quality for quantity. The supermarket replaced the farmers' market. And many folks sought out more exotic flavors from faraway lands, eschewing the treasures in their own backyard. It took a tragedy for many to see that America and Americana was slipping away.

In the years following 2001, things have slowly shifted. There are still mass-produced goods, but there's been a rise of handcrafted items and sites like Etsy where they can be sold. Locally owned bakeries, cafés, coffeeshops and restaurants, many

An interesting feature of labels of spirits from Ironclad Distillery Company in Newport News are blueprints of Civil War ironclads, which battled in the waterways just offshore from where the spirits are crafted. *Ironclad Distillery Company.*

utilizing locally sourced items, have sprang up, with appeal that takes a chink out of many chain eateries' armor. Folks still shop at supermarkets, but a number of neighborhoods now have their own farmers' markets.

Across the country and across the Commonwealth, there has been a significant rise in locally owned and operated breweries and wineries, as well as in distilleries. Indeed, since the turn of the twenty-first century, there's been a true Virginia spirits renaissance.

VIRGINIA'S SPIRITS RENAISSANCE

Notwithstanding A. Smith Bowman, which began making bourbon in Virginia immediately following Prohibition in 1933 and was the only legal whiskey distillery in Virginia until some point in the 1950s, there wasn't a lot of whiskey production in the state. Bowman, the state's oldest distillery, remained the only licensed distillery in Virginia for years. Of course, there was always someone making moonshine, but Virginians who wanted legal spirits only had one choice for many years.

Signs of what was to come began in 1988 when the husband-and-wife team of Chuck and Jeanette Miller renovated an old workshop and

Checking out the barrels at A. Smith Bowman in Fredericksburg, the oldest distillery in Virginia. *A. Smith Bowman Distillery.*

turned it into Belmont Farm Distillery in Culpeper. Chuck, inspired by his grandfather, who made illegal moonshine back in the day, began making legal Virginia Lightning. The whiskey is distilled in a 1930s copper pot and is highly lauded to this day.

It would be more than a decade before other distilleries opened. One pioneer was Richmond-based Cirrus Vodka, which opened in 2004. Still in operation today, award-winning Cirrus produces a premium, triple-filtered vodka. Another leader was Copper Fox Distillery, which opened in Sperryville in 2005 producing American whiskey, and it has since opened a second location in Williamsburg. Today, distiller Rick Wasmund offers a number of varieties of whiskey, including bourbon and rye variants.

The next year, in 2006, Chesapeake Bay Distillery's Chris Richeson began producing vodka in Virginia Beach. A few years later, the distillery moved from its original home in an industrial park to the ViBe Creative Arts District near the Oceanfront, offering a tasting room. A wide array of products is offered today, including a joint collaboration with the book's author, Four Farthing Spiced Rum.

Others would open over time, but it would still be a while before the spirits renaissance in the Old Dominion truly began. Based on successful legislation

Bottling bourbon at Ironclad Distillery Company in Newport News. *Ironclad Distillery Company.*

that had benefited Virginia's wineries, the General Assembly revised laws and regulations regarding distilleries. It worked, spurring growth.

In 2014, there were six licensed craft distilleries in Virginia. Today, there are about five dozen. About half of the distilleries are represented in statewide ABC (Alcohol Beverage Control) stores. Due to the COVID-19 pandemic, ABC rules began allowing distilleries to offer curbside pickup, home delivery within a certain radius of the distillery and shipping of product; check with each distillery for details.

FIVE DISTILLERS SHARE THEIR VISION

Twenty years into the twentieth century, with some five dozen distilleries producing award-winning spirits across the Commonwealth, what's there to look forward to? As A. Smith Bowman master distiller Brian Prewitt noted:

Virginia, like all other states, will play a role in the changing spirits scene. I would say that we are fortunate that there are several quality producers in the state. As consumer education and expectations rise, those who don't make a high-quality product shouldn't expect to be successful with the rising competition.

On what the future holds for Virginia spirits, I feel that Virginia will continue to have a strong distillation industry and there will be many more small distilleries that continue to open. Competition will be tight for all distilleries, and they will have to continue to evolve to consumer tastes and maintain product quality.

Those who don't will likely not make it. I hope that the industry doesn't experience the same sort of bubble that has happened in the brewing industry twice already. Hopefully, Virginia distillers will continue to delight and amaze their customers and provide a long and successful industry within the state.

Owen King, Ironclad Distillery's head distiller in Newport News, agreed:

Everyone always looks to Kentucky or Tennessee and thinks that's where the best whiskey is coming from, but we have quite a few distilleries that can go toe to toe with any of them.

The only thing Kentucky and Tennessee have on Virginia is age, but Virginia is rapidly catching up to them. If you look at blind tasting competitions, there is always a Virginia whiskey or spirit in the top five.

Autographed barrels full of bourbon at Ironclad Distillery Company in Newport News. *Ironclad Distillery Company.*

Our industry is growing rapidly, and we look forward to establishing Virginia as a state recognized for some of the best spirits produced in America.

But Dave Cuttino, owner and distiller of Reservoir Distillery in Richmond, thinks that Virginia has the birthright—it's just for the state to claim it and use to its advantage:

From the very first colonists to today, Virginia has a long history of entrepreneurs, and distilling is one of them....Every new distiller that joins us using Virginia grains and trees to make whiskey further establishes the Commonwealth as a distinct region of whiskey production in flavor and style. Much like the distinct regions of Scotland, the U.S. will continue to differentiate its regions, and Virginia holds a special spot given not only its flavor but its place in the history of distilling in America.

And it's not just Virginia's history; the hospitality and diversity of the state will play into its favor, said Karl Dornemann, Reverend Spirits owner and master distiller in Norfolk:

Virginians have long a history of being self-developing, relying on each other. Our biggest strength is our camaraderie and belief that together, we are stronger. Our southern hospitality strives to push everyone forward.

Also, Virginia is wonderfully dynamic with a wide range of geography and the people inhabiting those areas. That diversity also gives us a range of the types of spirits created. For example, older, more traditional spirits in older historical areas in the Blue Ridge, Mount Vernon and the like versus the more industrial areas of Virginia producing newer more adventurous types of spirits.

There are other assets Virginia has as well, noted Randy Thomas, Caiseal Beer & Spirits Company president in Hampton:

The craft spirits scene today is evolving through creativity and innovation. Virginia craft distillers are producing unique products that are changing perceptions about complete sub-categories of spirits, such as gin.

Previously, one of the lowest-volume spirits sub-categories, gin is now rapidly gaining popularity as craft distillers introduce new flavor profiles and aging techniques. Similarly, the establishment of American Single Malt

An unusual spirit from
Caiseal Bear & Spirits
Company in Hampton is
one distilled from grain from
previously brewed IPA beer.
Caiseal Beer & Spirits Company.

*Commission and producer's guidelines for American Single Malt Whiskey
illustrates growing enthusiasm for new products and styles.*

*I see the creation of new sub-categories of spirits and a blurring of lines
between traditional sub-categories becoming the norm as craft producers
push boundaries and expectations.*

*I also predict it will not be long before a discussion of "Single Malt"
in the United States will involve descriptions of vanilla, caramel, fruit
and spices rather than peat and smoke that we often relate to Scotch single
malt whisky.*

THE DISTILLERIES OF THE OLD DOMINION

From the first recorded distillation of spirits by colonist George Thorpe
at Berkeley Plantation in 1620—which led to America's first bourbon—
through to the heady days of rum production, illicit crafting of moonshine,
the dark days of Prohibition and the bright days of a renewed interest in

spirits, Virginia distillers have waxed and waned and waxed again. Virginia is truly the birthplace of American craft spirits, with distilleries across the Commonwealth.

Here is a list, as of press time, along with the type of spirit being produced; check with the distilleries themselves for any updates.

A. SMITH BOWMAN
asmithbowman.com
540-373-4555
1 Bowman Drive, Fredericksburg
Spirits: apple brandy, bourbon and variants, gin, rum, rye

BELLE ISLE MOONSHINE
belleislecraftspirits.com
804-723-1030
615 Maury Street, Richmond
Spirits: moonshine and flavored variants

BELMONT FARM DISTILLERY
belmontfarmdistillery.com
540-825-3207
13490 Cedar Run Road, Culpeper
Spirits: gin, vodka, moonshine, whiskey and variants

Of note: Belmont Farm Distillery is also home to Climax Moonshine from legendary distiller and star of Discovery Channel's Moonshiners *television series Tim Smith.*

BLUE SKY DISTILLERY
blueskydistillery.com
757-746-8342
20042 Isle of Wight Industrial Park Road, Smithfield
Spirits: vodka, rum, whiskey and variants

BONDURANT BROTHERS DISTILLERY
bondurantbrothersdistillery.com
434-738-7372
9 East Third Street, Chase City
Spirits: moonshine

CAISEAL BEER & SPIRITS COMPANY
caiseal.com
757-224-1216
504 North King Street, Hampton
Spirits: gin, vodka, single malt and "Whitestone
    Spirit"

The gin offering from
Caiseal Beer & Spirits
Company in Hampton.
*Caiseal Beer & Spirits
Company.*

CAPE CHARLES DISTILLERY
capecharlesdistillery.com
757-291-8016
222 Mason Avenue, Cape Charles
Spirits: vodka, moonshine, bourbon, whiskey and variants

CATOCTIN CREEK DISTILLING
catoctincreekdistilling.com
540-751-8404
120 West Main Street, Purcellville
Spirits: gin, rye whiskey, brandy and flavored variants

CHESAPEAKE BAY DISTILLERY
chesapeakebaydistillery.com
757-498-4210
437 Virginia Beach Boulevard, Virginia Beach
Spirits: Four Farthing Spiced Rum, vodka, rum, herb whiskey, lemon liqueur,
    agave tequila and variants

*Note: Visit FourFarthingSpicedRum.com for historical notes on that product and
specific recipes.*

CIRRUS VODKA
cirrusvodka.com
844-724-7787
1603 Ownby Lane, Richmond
Spirits: vodka

COPPER FOX DISTILLERY
copperfoxdistillery.com
540-987-8554
9 River Lane, Sperryville
Spirits: gin, bourbon, rye whiskey, single malt and variants

Note: There is a second distillery location at 901 Capitol Landing Road in Williamsburg.

DAVIS VALLEY DISTILLERY
davisvalleydistillery.com
276-686-8855
1167 Davis Valley Road, Rural Retreat
Spirits: vodka, moonshine, whiskey and variants

DEVIL'S BACKBONE DISTILLING COMPANY
dbbrewingcompany.com/distilling
540-817-6080
50 Northwind Lane, Lexington
Spirits: gin, rum and brandy

DIDA'S DISTILLERY
didasdistillery.com
540-551-8141
14437 Hume Road, Huntly
Spirits: brandy, gin and variants, vodka

DOME & SPEAR DISTILLERY
domeandspear.com
434-851-5477
4529 Dearborn Road, Evington
Spirits: bourbon

DRY FORK FRUIT DISTILLERY
dryforkdistillery.com
434-857-2337
534 Bridge Street, Danville
Spirits: moonshine, brandy and variants

EIGHT SHIRES COLONIALE DISTILLERY
8shires.com
757-378-2456
7218 C Merrimac Trail, Suite C, Williamsburg
Spirits: gin, rum, bourbon and variants

FALLS CHURCH DISTILLERS
fcdistillers.com
703-858-9186
442 South Washington Street, Suite A, Falls Church
Spirits: gin, vodka, rum, bourbon, whiskey, brandy and variants

FILIBUSTER DISTILLERY
filibusterbourbon.com
202-289-1414
80 Maurertown Mill Road, Maurertown
Spirits: gin, bourbon, whiskey and variants

FIVE MILE MOUNTAIN DISTILLERY
5milemountain.com
540-745-4495
489 Floyd Highway South, Floyd
Spirits: moonshine and variants

FRANKLIN COUNTY DISTILLERIES
franklincountydistilleries.com
540-334-1610
25156 Highway 220, Boones Mill
Spirits: rum, whiskey, brandy and flavored variants

GEORGE WASHINGTON'S DISTILLERY
mountvernon.org/the-estate-gardens/distillery
703-780-2000
5514 Mount Vernon Memorial Highway, Mount Vernon
Spirits: rye whiskey, brandy and variants

IRONCLAD DISTILLERY
ironcladdistillery.com
757-245-1996
124 Twenty-Third Street, Newport News
Spirits: bourbon, whiskey and variants

Bourbon offerings from Ironclad Distillery Company in Newport News. *Ironclad Distillery Company.*

JAMES RIVER DISTILLERY
jrdistillery.com
804-716-5172
2700 Hardy Street, Richmond
Spirits: gin, vodka, rum and "Oster Vit"

KO DISTILLING
kodistilling.com
571-292-1115
10381 Central Park Drive, Suite 105, Manassas
Spirits: gin, bourbon, rye and whiskey variants

LAW'S CHOICE WHEAT WHISKEY
lawschoice.com
540-489-3642
285 Laws Haven Lane, Rocky Mount
Spirits: wheat whiskey

LOST WHISKEY
lostwhiskey.com
202-438-3794
2811 Merrilee Drive, Suite D, Fairfax
Spirits: rye-heavy bourbon, wheat-heavy bourbon

MONTE PICCOLO
montepiccolo.com
434-305-7979
3135 Blandemar Drive, Charlottesville
Spirits: gin, brandy and flavored variants

MOUNT DEFIANCE CIDERY & DISTILLERY
mtdefiance.com
540-687-8100
207 West Washington Street, Middleburg
Spirits: absinthe, almond liqueur, amaretto, cassis liqueur, rum, bourbon,
    brandy, vermouth and variants

MURLARKEY DISTILLED SPIRITS
murlarkey.com
571-284-7961
7961 Gainsford Court, Bristow
Spirits: gin, vodka, whiskey and variants

OLD HOUSE VINEYARDS
oldhousevineyards.com
540-423-1032
18351 Corkys Lane, Culpeper
Spirits: moonshine

RAGGED BRANCH
raggedbranch.com
434-244-2600
1075 Taylors Gap Road, Charlottesville
Spirits: bourbon, rye whiskey and variants

RESERVOIR DISTILLERY
reservoirdistillery.com
804-912-2621
1800 Summit Avenue, Richmond
Spirits: bourbon, rye whiskey, wheat whiskey and variants

REVEREND SPIRITS
drinkreverend.com
757-233-9168
1120 West Olney Road, Norfolk
Spirits: bourbon, gin, vodka

RIVER HILL WINE & SPIRITS
riverhilldistillery.com
540-843-0890
356 Ruffners Ferry Road, Luray
Spirits: bourbon and corn whiskey

SILVERBACK DISTILLERY
sbdistillery.com
540-456-7070
9374 Rockfish Valley Highway, Afton
Spirits: gin, bourbon, rye whiskey and variants

Sleepy Fox Distillery
sleepyfoxdistillery.com
804-525-0628
266 North Washington Highway, Ashland
Spirits: moonshine and flavored variants, vodka, bourbon and maple whiskey

Spirit Lab Distilling
spiritlabdistilling.com
434-218-2605
1503 Sixth Street Southeast, Suite 2, Charlottesville
Spirits: gin, single malt and variants

Springfield Distillery
springfielddistillery.com
434-575-9317
9040 River Road, Halifax
Spirits: rum, bourbon and corn whiskey

Stone Mountain Distilling
facebook.com/stonemountaindistilling
276-970-4081
2219 East Main Street, Lebanon
Spirits: moonshine and variants

Tarnished Truth Distilling Company
tarnishedtruth.com
757-965-9652
4200 Atlantic Avenue, Virginia Beach
Spirits: gin, vodka, moonshine, bourbon, rye whiskey and whiskey cream

Three Brothers Distillery
threebrotherswhiskey.com
757-204-1357
9935 County Line Road, Disputanta
Distiller: David Reavis
Spirits: gin, corn whiskey and rye whiskey

THREE CROSSES DISTILLING COMPANY
threecrossesdistilling.com
804-818-6330
3835 Old Buckingham Road, Suite A, Powhatan
Spirits: vodka, moonshine, rum, whiskey and variants

TRIAL AND ERROR
trialanderrordistillery.com
804-213-0212
1606 West Main Street, Richmond
Spirits: gin, rum, grappa and variants

TWIN CREEKS DISTILLERY
twincreeksdistillery.com
540-483-1266
510 Franklin Street, Rocky Mount
Spirits: moonshine, white whiskey, brandy and variants

VIRAGO SPIRITS
viragospirits.com
804-355-8746
1727 Rhoadmiller Street, Richmond
Spirits: rum and variants

VIRGINIA DISTILLERY COMPANY
vadistillery.com
434-285-2900
299 Eades Lane, Lovingston
Spirits: "Virginia Highland Whisky" and variants

VITAE SPIRITS DISTILLERY
vitaespirits.com
434-270-0317
715 Henry Avenue, Charlottesville
Spirits: anisette, rum, gin, flavored liqueurs and variants

RECIPES

During the past two decades of the twenty-first century, several trends have come and gone in the world of cocktails, and some seem like they are here to stay. Americans, including Virginians, turn their palates not just from the plate but to the glass, looking for locally sourced ingredients in many instances. Others have stretched the boundaries of cocktails to a degree or two, incorporating non-traditional ingredients such as vegetables, beyond the obvious bloody mary.

Relaxed ABC laws have also allowed bartenders to experiment more, opening up opportunities to infuse spirits with such items ranging from herbs and spices to fruits and vegetables and even candy. Folks have moved their passion for drinks from beyond brunch, lunch, happy hour and dinner to dessert as well.

Two other trends in the twenty-first century include mocktails, or cocktails that are made without alcohol, and barrel-aged cocktails. For barrel-aged, drinks are made and placed in a small cask for a short period of time, allowing the flavors to meld. Cocktail aging kits, which include an aging barrel, are available at certain boutique shops, which sell cocktail and spirit-related items, and also online.

File this under "everything old is new again": another trend involves the return of the classics. Folks craved authentic, well-crafted drinks, and bartenders have been all too happy to shake, stir and serve them up in classy glassware and with artful garnishes. On the revival menu: boulevardiers, martinis, Manhattans, negronis, old fashioneds and more.

WE GOT THE BEET-INI

This brilliantly red, vodka-based martini follows the trend of using a non-traditional ingredient, in this case beets. Earthy notes from the root vegetable play with the spice from the ginger and the muted sweetness from the pear in the drink, amped up with a premium Virginia vodka.

Note: You could use 1 ounce of juice from a jar of pickled beets and 1 ounce of juice from a can of pear juice if you prefer rather than making the beet/pear juice from scratch.

Ginger Simple Syrup Ingredients
1 3-inch piece fresh ginger
1 cup sugar
1 cup water

Beet Ingredients
2 pounds small whole beets, trimmed
3 tablespoons olive oil

Beet Juice Ingredients
roasted, diced beets
2 medium pears, seeds removed and diced (retain a few thin slices first for garnishes)
½ cup water
1 ounce ginger simple syrup

Cocktail Ingredients
2 ounces beet/pear juice
2 ounces vodka
½ ounce ginger simple syrup
½ ounce freshly squeezed lemon juice
thin pear slice for garnish

To make the simple syrup, peel the skin from the piece of ginger and slice into thin disks. In a small saucepan over medium-high heat, add the ginger, sugar and water and bring to a boil, stirring occasionally, until sugar is dissolved. Remove from heat and allow to cool to room temperature. Strain and add to a sealable glass jar and refrigerate until use, up to 1 month.

To make the beets, preheat the oven to 375 degrees Fahrenheit. Place the beets on a tinfoil-lined baking sheet and toss with the olive oil to coat. Cover the beets with another sheet of tinfoil and crimp the edges of both pieces to seal. Roast the beets for 20–25 minutes, then check for doneness by inserting the tip of a knife into a beet; it should easily slip in. Roast longer if needed, checking for doneness every 5–10 minutes. Remove the beets from oven and allow to cool. When the beets are cool enough to handle, slip the skin off with your fingers or remove with a paring knife. Slice the cooled, roasted beets into ¼-inch slices and set aside.

To make the beet/pear juice, place the beets and pears in a blender with about a half cup water and 1 ounce of the prepared ginger simple syrup and process until smooth. Pour into a fine strainer and push through into a container below. Add water, stirring constantly, until a juice forms. There should be enough juice for several cocktails; reserve any leftovers in a sealable glass jar and refrigerate until use, up to 1 week.

To make the cocktail, in a cocktail shaker add 2 ounces of beet/pear juice, 2 ounces of vodka, ½ ounce ginger syrup and ½ ounce freshly squeezed lemon juice. Fill with ice and shake vigorously. Strain into a martini glass and garnish with a thin pear slice.

Yields 1 cocktail.

STORM'S BREWIN'
(WITH CATEGORY FIVE MOONSHINE CHERRIES)

Punches have always been a favorite drink in Virginia, but large-format drinks served in pitchers are following new trends. We take a little bit of the old and a little bit of the new with our Storm's Brewin', designed for a sixty-four-ounce pitcher to serve eight thirsty folks.

It's our Virginia-fied take on the classic New Orleans hurricane. In fact, when hurricane creator Pat O'Brien was running a speakeasy in the Crescent City, the password was Storm's Brewin'. Certainly, Coastal Virginia has a long history with hurricanes, nor'easters and other storms, as well as trade with the Caribbean, which is why we swap out the hard-to-find passionfruit juice in the original for the more apropos pineapple juice. Also, pineapples have long been a symbol of Virginia hospitality.

Cocktail Ingredients
16 ounces dark or spiced rum
16 ounces white rum
12 ounces pineapple juice
8 ounces fresh squeezed orange juice
8 ounces fresh squeezed lime juice
4 ounces grenadine syrup
3–4 oranges, sliced
moonshine cherries

Moonshine Cherry Ingredients
1 pound cherries, pitted (such as Bing)
1 orange peel, cut into thick strips
1 pint clear corn whiskey, such as moonshine

To make the cocktail, in a sixty-four-ounce pitcher, combine the dark/white rum, pineapple juice, orange juice, lime juice and grenadine. Stir to incorporate. Add half the orange sliced and refrigerate for 2–3 hours, or until chilled.

To prepare the cherries, combine the cherries and orange peel in a pint jar. Pour the whiskey over the top to completely cover the cherries. Seal and shake slightly; allow the cherries to steep at room temperature for at least 72 hours before using. Stored in a sealed jar in the refrigerator, the cherries will keep for up to 3 months.

To make the individual cocktails, pour cocktail into individual glasses filled with ice and garnish with remaining orange slices. Skewer several moonshine cherries and add to glass. Yields 8 cocktails.

G + K (GIN + KOMBUCHA)

Fermentation has been a hot commodity the past few years—just about everything that could be pickled has been pickled. And it's reached farther than that to unusual vinegars and other liquids too. One of the more popular beverages in this realm in the twenty-first century has been kombucha.

Kombucha starts with black or green tea that is sweetened. The tea is fermented and takes on a light effervescence. Often there are additives and flavorings to the kombucha, such as juice and spices. Kombucha is reported to have a variety of health benefits, but many folks drink it for its flavor, which often has a pleasant sourness to it due to the fermentation process.

Our G + K cocktail is a light, refreshing drink that can be different each time you make it depending on the flavor of kombucha you pick; we like something with floral notes.

2 ounces gin
1 tablespoon freshly squeezed lime juice
1 ½ teaspoons simple syrup

2–4 ounces kombucha
lime wedge

In a cocktail shaker add gin, lime juice and simple syrup; fill with ice, close and shake vigorously. Fill an old fashioned glass with ice and pour cocktail shaker contents inside. Top with kombucha and garnish with lime wedge. Yields 1 cocktail.

BOYS TO THE YARD BOOZY MILKSHAKE (WITH BOURBON WHIPPED CREAM)

The '90s gave us myriad non-traditional martinis, among them the espresso-tini and other sweet drinks that could double as dessert.

Bourbon Whipped Cream Ingredients
1 cup heavy whipping cream
⅓ cup confectioners' sugar
2 teaspoons bourbon or other whiskey

Milkshake Ingredients
1 cup premium chocolate ice cream
1 cup ice
½ cup milk
3 ounces bourbon or other whiskey
1 ounce chocolate syrup
chocolate shavings for garnish
moonshine cherries (see method under the Storm's Brewin' recipe)

To make the whipped cream, chill a medium metal bowl and a metal whisk a few hours beforehand. In the bowl pour the heavy whipping cream along with the sugar and bourbon/whiskey. Whisk vigorously until soft peaks form, about 5 minutes. Cover and refrigerate until ready for use; use soon.

To make the milkshakes, in a blender add the ice cream, ice, milk, bourbon/whiskey, and chocolate syrup and blend on low. Slowly increase blender speed until mixture has reached a smooth consistency, about 2–3 minutes; add additional milk if you want a thinner milkshake.

To assemble the milkshakes, pour prepared milkshakes into two tall glasses and top with a generous amount of prepared whipped cream. Garnish with chocolate shavings and a moonshine cherry. Yields 2 cocktails.

CARIBBEAN QUEEN SPRITZ

A growing trend beginning in the 2010s became the in-house infusion of spirits. Sure, mixologists and home bartenders alike could purchase vanilla-flavored vodka, but how much better to make your own with real vanilla beans and no artificial ingredients added?

Better yet, how much better to create your own unique flavor profiles, like bacon-jalapeño vodka, perfect for use in bloody marys? One of our favorite infusions is also one of the easiest to do: pineapple-infused vodka. The pineapple adds an exotic note and understated sweetness to the vodka, while harkening to Virginia's rich ties to the Caribbean and the use of the fruit as a symbol of hospitality in the state for centuries. There are many uses for the pineapple-infused vodka, including marvelous tropical martinis and killer piña coladas, but we like a simple spritz, outlined here.

Look for more vodka and other spirit-infused recipes on our companion website, virginiadistilled.com, or at virginiaeatsanddrinks.com.

Pineapple-Infused Vodka Ingredients
1 medium fresh pineapple
1 750ml bottle vodka

Cocktail Ingredients
3 ounces pineapple vodka
seltzer water
vodka-soaked pineapple chunks
fresh mint

To make the infused vodka, with a sharp chef's knife remove the pineapple crown and a small bit of the bottom so it sits evenly. Stand the pineapple upright and, working from the top down, follow the curve of the fruit to remove the peel in several slices. With a small paring knife, remove the eyes and any other small hard spots. With a chef's knife, cut the pineapple into quarters lengthwise and then remove the inner part of each piece that contains the hard core. Cut each piece into approximate 1-by-1-inch chunks and place in a large, sealable glass container. Pour in the vodka, seal and let steep in the refrigerator for 2 weeks.

To make the cocktail, in a tall glass filled with ice, add the pineapple vodka and fill with seltzer water. Take several vodka-soaked pineapple chunks from the infusion container and skewer, laying across the top of the glass horizontally as a garnish. Add a sprig of mint for an additional garnish. Yields 1 cocktail.

QUARANTINI

It wouldn't be a chapter about the twenty-first century without talking about perhaps the biggest news stories of 2020: the COVID-19 pandemic.

In an unprecedented move, the Virginia Alcohol Beverage Control made spirits much more accessible to folks while they were quarantined at home through options such as home delivery from distilleries and curbside pickup at distilleries.

Throughout the year, folks posted photos on social media of their "quarantini" cocktail, as happy hour started earlier into the day and stretched later into the evening. Looking at all the posts, one thing was clear: everyone's idea of what constituted a quarantini was as diverse as Virginia itself. Everyone was improvising with whatever spirits and other ingredients they had on hand and making do with whatever pleased their palate but calling it the same name: quarantini.

I developed two basic formulas utilizing ingredients many folks had on hand for an easy, delicious and quick drink. One is an overly simplistic version of a daiquiri and one an old fashioned.

Clear Spirits Quarantini
3 ounces clear spirit such as gin, moonshine, white rum or vodka
1 ½ ounces freshly squeezed citrus juice such as grapefruit, lemon or lime

½ ounce simple syrup
fresh fruit slice (same as juice) to garnish

Pour spirit, juice and simple syrup in a cocktail shaker and fill with ice. Shake vigorously and strain into a martini glass. Garnish with a fresh fruit slice. Yields 1 cocktail.

Dark Spirits Quarantini
2 strips of citrus peel from fruit as grapefruit, lemon, or lime
2 maraschino cherries or moonshine cherries (for moonshine cherries, see method
under Storm's Brewin' recipe)
1 teaspoon granulated sugar
1 teaspoon water
3 ounces dark spirit such as bourbon or other whiskey like rye or dark/spiced rum
fresh fruit slice (same as juice) and additional cherries to garnish

Twist the citrus peel over an old fashioned glass and add to the glass. Add 2 cherries and 1 teaspoon sugar and water. With a muddler or the handle of a wooden spoon, press down on the fruit and work around until fruit breaks up and sugar is dissolved in the water and fruit pulp. Add ice and spirit and stir for a minute or two to make sure the spirit gets chilled. Garnish with fruit slice and additional cherries on a skewer. Yields 1 cocktail.

Chapter 6

RESOURCES

Places important in relation to the content of this book.

DISTILLERIES

For a list of current Virginia distilleries, see chapter 5.

Engraving of the Apollo Room interior by American historian Benson Lossing, circa 1850. *Author's collection.*

Taverns and Ordinaries

By the mid-seventeenth century, places for travelers to lodge overnight and grab a bite to eat and drink began popping up in Virginia, mirroring, in many ways, aspects of the inns, pubs, ordinaries and taverns the colonists had left behind in England. But taverns filled many needs in Colonial America—not just as a place for food, beverage and lodging but also as a social gathering place and space for exchanging information and ideas.

Across the Commonwealth, there are still taverns from colonial times that operate as restaurants or are open as historic sites.

The Boyd Tavern
Circa 1790
boydtavern.net
434-738-9800
449 Washington Street, Boydton

The Boyd Tavern—also known as Boyd's Tavern, Exchange Hotel and Boydton Hotel—was originally opened as an ordinary to serve eats and drinks and provide lodging. The original tavern was operated by Richard Swepson Jr. Today, the historical building is open for tours.

Boykins Tavern
Circa 1780
historicisleofwight.com/boykins-tavern
757-357-5182
17130 Monument Circle, Isle of Wight

Francis Boykin served as a lieutenant with Patrick Henry (who was a "barkeeper" according to Thomas Jefferson, before he became a Founding Father) and was with George Washington at Valley Forge during the American Revolution. He purchased land in Isle of Wight County, just west of Smithfield, donated a portion for the county courthouse and established a tavern. Today, the historical building is open for tours.

CHOWNINGS'S TAVERN
Reconstructed eighteenth-century building in Colonial Williamsburg
colonialwilliamsburghotels.com
855-270-5114
109 East Duke of Gloucester Street, Williamsburg

Chowning's Tavern is open for meal service with period-inspired dishes. Josiah Chowning operated the tavern on the Court House Green as an alehouse, as announced in the *Virginia Gazette* on October 10, 1766. Two years later, it changed hands; new owner William Elliot promised "all Gentlemen…good accommodation for themselves, servants, and horses, and the best entertainment."

CHRISTIANA CAMPBELL TAVERN
Reconstructed eighteenth-century building in Colonial Williamsburg
colonialwilliamsburghotels.com
855-263-1746
101 South Waller Street, Williamsburg

Christiana Campbell Tavern is open for meal service with period-inspired dishes. Campbell kept her tavern from 1755 through the next ten years or so to provide income for herself and her daughters following her husband's death. Among her notable patrons were Thomas Jefferson and George Washington, who, tradition says, favored seafood here.

FERRY PLANTATION HOUSE
Circa 1850
ferryplantationva.net
757-473-5182
4136 Cheswick Lane, Virginia Beach

Ferry Plantation House—also known as Old Donation Farm, Ferry Farm and Walke Manor House—has ties back to 1642, when early ferry service in the region began here. The current 1850 house morphed over time from previous structures dating back to the early eighteenth century that had been added to, and burned and built on the foundations of previous structures. It has been used as a courthouse, plantation and school, as well as for other functions. The trial of Grace Sherwood, the only Virginian convicted of witchcraft, took place here in 1706. Eleven ghosts haunt the property.

Archaeological digs at the Ferry Plantation House have found evidence of a seventeenth-century tavern at the property, although there are no remains left today. Today, the historical building is open for tours.

HANOVER TAVERN
Circa 1791
hanovertavern.org
804-537-5050
13181 Hanover Courthouse Road, Hanover

The current 1791 building, one of the oldest taverns in the United States, is part of a courthouse complex that was established in 1733 that included Shelton Tavern. The tavern was owned by John Shelton, who was father-in-law of Patrick Henry, who made his famous "Give me liberty or give me death" speech nearby. Before Henry became a Virginia governor and a Founding Father of the country, he worked at the tavern, doing a number of tasks, among them tending bar.

Today, the Hanover Tavern is open for tours, and an adjacent restaurant offers specialties including Rappahannock (Virginia) fried oysters, smoked ham dip made with Virginia ham, Chesapeake-style lump crab cakes and shrimp and grits crafted with locally stone-ground Byrd's Mill grits. The Barksdale Theatre is also attached.

KING'S ARMS TAVERN
Reconstructed eighteenth-century building in Colonial Williamsburg
colonialwilliamsburghotels.com
855-240-3278
416 East Duke of Gloucester Street, Williamsburg

King's Arms Tavern is open for meal service with period-inspired dishes. Jane Vobe, who promised "good eating" in a place "where the best people resorted," opened the original King's Arms Tavern in 1772.

Postcard showing interior of the King's Arms Tavern in Williamsburg. Note the straightaway wooden area where the tavernkeeper made drinks, or bar. *Author's collection.*

MICHIE TAVERN
Circa 1784
michietavern.com
434-977-1234
683 Thomas Jefferson Parkway, Charlottesville

Originally established in the Albemarle County community of Earlysville in 1784, Michie Tavern was purchased and moved a short distance to its present location, a half mile from Thomas Jefferson's Monticello. Present day, the tavern is open for tours and serves a period-inspired menu, with dishes including southern fried chicken, hickory-smoked pork barbecue, black-eyed peas seasoned with country ham, stewed tomatoes, buttermilk biscuits, cornbread and more. There is also a pub with Virginia beer, cider and wine among its offerings. A tavern shop is located next to the ordinary.

R. CHARLTON'S COFFEEHOUSE
Reconstructed eighteenth-century building in Colonial Williamsburg
colonialwilliamsburg.com
888-965-7254
429 East Duke of Gloucester Street, Williamsburg

R. Charlton's Coffeehouse is open for tours with samples of period-inspired (drinking) chocolate and coffee. Opened in the early 1760s by Richard Charlton, the coffeehouse operated for a decade, serving the likes of George Washington and Thomas Jefferson. Located near the capitol, it was a center of activity.

RALEIGH TAVERN
Reconstructed eighteenth-century building in Colonial Williamsburg
colonialwilliamsburg.com
888-965-7254
413 East Duke of Gloucester Street, Williamsburg

Raleigh Tavern operates as a museum and is open for tours. This was one of the largest taverns in Colonial Virginia, and the Apollo Room, a large

Raleigh Tavern, Williamsburg, circa 1940. *Author's collection.*

banquet hall within, saw many famous Patriots pass through, including Patrick Henry. Above the mantel was the Latin phrase *Hilaritas sapientiae et bonae vitae proles* ("Jollity is the offspring of wisdom and good living"). Adjacent is a bakery with colonial-inspired light lunch items and baked goods, as well as hot cider.

RED FOX INN AND TAVERN
Circa 1728
redfox.com
540-687-6301
2 East Washington Street, Middleburg

Serving as a boutique inn, restaurant and special events venue, Red Fox Inn and Tavern began as Chinn's Ordinary. The imposing fieldstone structure is located in downtown Middleburg, the unofficial capital of Virginia's Hunt Country. Look for such Virginia-centric menu items in the tavern as house smoked rainbow trout on toast as a starter, Virginia peanut soup, crab cakes and Duroc pork chops served with spicy plum Virginia chutney.

The Red Fox Inn and Tavern, Middleburg, circa 1935. The Red Fox has been a mainstay in Virginia's Hunt Country since 1728. *Author's collection.*

RICE'S HOTEL/HUGHLETT'S TAVERN
Circa 1795
rhhtfoundationinc.org
804-580-3377
73 Monument Place, Heathsville

One of the oldest surviving wooden structures on Virginia's Northern Neck, the Rice's Hotel/Hughlett's Tavern started as a three-room tavern built by John Hughlett in the late 1700s. Today, it is home to four artisan guilds, the Heritage Arts Center, a gift shop and the Tavern Café, offering lunch and sweets various days of the week.

SCHWARTZ TAVERN
Circa 1798
434-292-7795
100 Tavern Street, Blackstone

John Schwartz, an early settler in Nottoway County, opened a tavern at this spot in the late eighteenth century. The building has been altered over the years. Today, the historical building is open for tours.

SHIELDS TAVERN
Reconstructed eighteenth-century building in Colonial Williamsburg
colonialwilliamsburghotels.com
855-268-7220
422 East Duke of Gloucester Street, Williamsburg

Shields Tavern is open for meal service with period-inspired dishes. Originally Marot's Ordinary, owned by John Marot, the property passed to his daughter, Anne, following his death and became Shields Tavern in 1705 after she married James Shields.

SMITHFIELD INN
Circa 1752
smithfieldinn.com
757-357-1752
112 Main Street, Smithfield

Located in downtown Smithfield, this building began life in 1752 as the William Rand Tavern, providing food and lodging. For much of the nineteenth century, it was owned by the Vestry of Christ Church. In 1922, Daniel Webster Sykes and his wife, Annie Mae, purchased the building and opened the Sykes Inn, providing food and lodging as William Rand originally did.

Today, the Smithfield Inn is located here; a restaurant and bar are located on the first floor, offering upscale southern-inspired menus, with guest rooms on the second story. Noted menu items include Smithfield Inn ham rolls, Brunswick stew, the Inn's Famous Crab Cakes and Smithfield pork and apple.

THE TAVERN
Circa 1779
276-628-1118
222 East Main Street, Abingdon

This site began as an inn and tavern in 1779 to serve stagecoach travelers traversing the passage through the Great Appalachian Valley. Over the years, it has hosted many guests, including President Andrew Jackson and King Louis Philippe of France. It has also served many functions, including general store, post office, private residence and more. During the Civil War, it was used as a hospital for both wounded Confederate and Union soldiers.

In 1994, it once again became a tavern, serving eats and drinks. A showstopper on the contemporary menu is the brie cheese appetizer, baked with honey, brown sugar and toasted almonds and served in a toasted bread bowl. In addition to more than a half dozen signature dishes, there are a number of German offerings as well, including jagerschnitzel and Wiener schnitzel, a nod to the owner's heritage.

Events and Other

Alexandria Old Town Cocktail Week

A weeklong springtime celebration of Alexandria's craft cocktail scene, with special cocktail menus at participating restaurants, seminars, tastings and in-store events.

visitalexandriava.com

Berkeley Plantation

One of the first plantations in the New World, Berkeley Plantation was established in 1619 along the shores of the James River between present-day Williamsburg and Richmond. It was here the first Thanksgiving in English-speaking America took place, as well as the first recorded distilled spirits when "corn beer" was crafted by colonist George Thorpe in 1620, a predecessor to modern-day bourbon. Berkeley Plantation is located at 12602 Harrison Landing Road, Charles City.

berkeleyplantation.com

Blue Ridge Whisky Wine Loop

The Blue Ridge Whisky Wine Loop is a travel plan through portions of the northern Blue Ridge Mountain region that includes recommended visits to a number of breweries, eateries, wineries and more. Also on the loop are stops at Copper Fox Distillery in Sperryville and River Hill Distillery in Luray.

discovershenandoah.com

Grape & Grains Trail

A curated self-paced tour across Northern Virginia, with stops at five wineries and A. Smith Bowman Distillery in Fredericksburg. A ticket includes tastings, commemorative glass and discounts on merchandise and wine purchases.

grapesandgrainstrail.com

All set up for a tasting of bourbon at Norfolk's Reverend Spirits. *Karl Dornemann of Reverend Spirits.*

DISTILLERY EVENTS AND TOURS

For a list of events and tours at Virginia distilleries, visit the individual distillery websites as listed in chapter 5.

REPEAL DAY

December 5 is the anniversary of the day Prohibition was repealed in 1933 with the ratification of the Twenty-First Amendment to the U.S. Constitution. President Franklin D. Roosevelt famously quipped, "What America needs now is a drink." And drink America—and Virginia—did. Look for Repeal Day events at local distilleries, restaurants and other venues on this special day. (We will have links on our *Virginia Distilled* companion website.)

virginiadistilled.com

SPIRITED VIRGINIA

The Virginia Alcoholic Beverage Control (ABC) Authority publishes the quarterly *Spirited Virginia* magazine with engaging articles regarding Virginia's craft spirits scene and beyond, including cocktail recipes and more. A print version of the magazine is available at ABC stores across the Commonwealth; an electronic version is available on ABC's website.

abc.virginia.gov

TOAST THE COAST: BEER, WINE AND SHINE TRAIL

Toast the Coast links spirited spots across Coastal Virginia, including breweries, distilleries, wineries and more, as a convenient resource for locals and visitors to the region. The trail was developed by the Newport News Tourism Development Office.

toastthecoastva.com

VIRGINIA CULINARY HALL OF FAME

Throughout its history, Virginia has been a leading tastemaker in food and foodways. Cooks and chefs, bartenders, farmers, watermen, winemakers, brewers, distillers, specialty food producers, advocates and enthusiasts and more have their story told in one place: the Virginia Culinary Hall of Fame.

Each year, new inductees are added to the hall of fame. At press time, two spirits-related persons are honorees: George Thorpe and John Dabney. For more information on Thorpe, see chapter 1. For more information on Dabney, see chapter 3.

virginiaculinaryhalloffame.com

VIRGINIA DISTILLED

This is a companion website for this book, with additional and behind-the-scene interviews, photos, reads, recipes, resources, tips and tricks. Also look for information about where the book is sold, as well as book signings, a select calendar of events listing, memorabilia and merchandise and more.

virginiadistilled.com
virginiaeatsanddrinks.com

VIRGINIA DISTILLERS ASSOCIATION

The Virginia Distillers Association (VDA) is an advertising and marketing association representing member distilleries across the Commonwealth in a number of ways.

Among public venues are periodic Virginia Spirits Roadshows, open-to-the-public events held at various locations throughout Virginia with numerous distilleries offering samples of spirits, as well as prepared cocktails.

Virginia Spirits Month special events are coordinated through the association each September. The association also coordinates the Virginia Spirits Trail, which embraces the old, the new and the high-proofed throughout Virginia's four-hundred-year history of spirits. Information is found online, and a print copy can be picked up at any participating Virginia distillery to learn more about the "Birthplace of American Spirits."

virginiaspirits.org

Chapter 7

EATS AND DRINKS-TIONARY

ALCOHOL AND RELATED

"angel's share": Alcohol stored in porous barrels that is lost to evaporation.

aqua vitae: Literally "water of life," an ancient term for a strong, often clear alcoholic spirit.

bathtub gin: A term popularized during Prohibition describing a homemade, usually poor-quality mixture of cheap, grain alcohol, water, flavorings and other ingredients. It is a common misconception that the name comes from the spirit being made in an actual bathtub; rather, it refers to the large bottles it was crafted in.

brandy: An alcoholic drink, sometimes aged in a wooden cask, that has been distilled from wine.

cask: A hollow, cylindrical vessel with bulging center, traditionally made of wooden staves held together with metal or wooden hoops, used to age and store items such as spirits. Also called a barrel.

cocktail: The Merriam-Webster Dictionary defines a cocktail as "A usually iced drink of wine or distilled liquor mixed with flavoring ingredients." But it's much more complicated than that. No doubt cocktails have evolved over

Manassas, Va.—Field Maneuvers, Sept., 1904. Soldiers Refreshing Themselves after a Hard Day's Work.

Soldiers refreshing themselves with some ardent spirits in September 1904 after field maneuvers in Manassas. *Author's collection.*

time, but they have been thriving for much longer than many folks realize—longer than the term was first put into use, either in 1798 or 1803, depending on which story you subscribe to.

It was in 1806 that the cocktail was not only mentioned but also defined for the first time, and it's a definition that holds true for many drinks even today. Harry Croswell, editor of the *Balance and Columbian Repository* in Hudson, New York, wrote, "Cock-tail is a stimulating liquor, composed of spirits of any kind, sugar, water, and bitters—it is vulgarly called bittered sling."

Although there were somewhat standard cocktail recipes about, it wasn't until 1862 that Professor Jerry Thomas published the first true cocktail recipe book, *How to Mix Drinks, or The Bon Vivant's Companion*, still a valuable guide in its own right.

What many consider to be the oldest, most classic cocktail is the old fashioned, which comprises a spirit (usually bourbon or rye whiskey), sugar, water and bitters; it may have appeared as early as the first quarter of the nineteenth century but had become well established by midcentury.

cordial: See "liqueur."

dry: With drinking, there are two meanings regarding the term "dry": the forbiddance of alcohol manufacture, distribution or sale, as in a dry county, or as during Prohibition; and the lack of sweetness, usually from lack of sugar, in an alcoholic beverage.

liqueur: Historically the offshoots of ancient herbal medicines dating back some seven hundred years, liqueurs, sometimes called cordials or schnapps, are distilled spirits with additives such as fruits, herbs, nuts, seeds and spices. They are often sweetened and usually served with dessert. Liqueurs can be offered straight, over ice, in coffee or as an ingredient in dishes.

liquor: An alcoholic beverage that has been distilled, such as whiskey, rather than fermented, such as wine.

moonshine: A high-proof distilled spirit so named because it is often made illicitly at nighttime under the shine of the moon. Check out chapter 4 for a list of moonshine lingo.

nip: A smaller portion or shot, such as alcohol. Also see "nip joint" in "Places."

pony: A smaller glass for liquor, traditionally holding one ounce.

spirit: An alcoholic drink produced by distillation.

virgin: A beverage, such as a cocktail, that does not contain any alcohol.

whisky/whiskey: All bourbon is whiskey, but not all whiskey is bourbon. Whiskey—a liquor crafted from barley, corn or rye mash—was probably first distilled as early as the sixteenth century, with Old Bushmills Distillery in Northern Ireland being the oldest licensed whiskey distillery in the world, coming on board in 1608. There are many variations of whiskey, including Canadian whisky, Irish whiskey, Japanese whiskey, Scotch and others.

In America, whiskey is made, but so is bourbon. In order for a whiskey to be called "bourbon," it must be made from a mash that is at least 51 percent corn and aged—for no particular amount of time—in new, charred oak barrels. The "corn beer" distilled by George Thorpe at Berkeley Plantation between Jamestown and Richmond in 1620 was a predecessor to modern-day bourbon.

EQUIPMENT, INCLUDING GLASSWARE

bar spoon: Used in bartending, this spoon is used in mixed drinks and is equivalent to a teaspoon.

Collins glass: This tall, narrow, cylindrical tumbler is used for cocktails like the Tom Collins and holds ten to fourteen fluid ounces. It is taller than a highball glass.

flask: A broad, flattened vessel fitted with a closure and a neck for easy drinking, used to transport alcohol on the person.

highball: This tall cylindrical tumbler is used for a number of cocktails and holds eight to twelve fluid ounces. It is taller than a lowball glass but shorter than a Collins glass. Also see "highball" in "Types of Drinks."

jigger: A small cup used to measure spirits in cocktails, usually holding one to two ounces. Also see "free pour" in "Processes and Procedures."

julep cup: A silver or tin cup used for serving mint juleps. The metal helps keep the drink cold and frosty, especially on a hot Virginia day. Contrary to popular belief, mint juleps are a creation of the Old Dominion and not Kentucky, where they are highly associated with the Kentucky Derby.

muddler: A pestle used by bartenders to mash fruits, herbs and spices in the bottom of a glass to release their flavor while a cocktail is being created, used in drinks such as the mint julep and the old fashioned. Also see "muddling" in "Types of Drinks."

shaker: A two-piece device used to mix alcoholic beverages and to quickly cool them when ice is added. Cocktail shakers are often tin; a Boston shaker is composed of a sixteen-ounce mixing glass and twenty-eight-ounce metal shaker tin.

shot glass: A small measured glass that holds a spirit or a mixture or spirits that are drunk from the glass or which are poured from the glass into another vessel. While there is no standard size shot in the United States, many are one and a half ounces. Also see "shot, shooter" in "Types of Drinks."

swizzle stick: A stick, often ornamental, used to stir cocktails. Swizzle sticks originated in the eighteenth century at a West Indies rum plantation using pieces from the swizzle stick tree, or *Quaraibea tubinata*, an aromatic, perineal shrub found throughout the Caribbean.

EVENTS

"Dark Ages of the Cocktail": A period that ran from approximately the late 1960s to the early 2000s when the focus was on drinks that were highly sugared or often frozen; shots were added; and classic drinks were eschewed. During this time, vodka often replaced other spirits in traditional drinks, like martinis; speaking of martinis, everything became a martini, from an espresso-tini to a green apple-tini.

"Platinum Age of the Cocktail": Many folks say that we are currently living in the platinum age due to the showcasing of talent of bartenders/mixologists, focus on craft sprits, resurgence of classic cocktails and innovation of creative cocktails.

Prohibition: Long before the national constitutional ban on the production, importation, transportation and sale of alcoholic beverages, there was a temperance movement in the United States advocating for a dry America. Crusaders successfully led to statewide and nationwide support of making beer, spirits and wine illegal under the Eighteenth Amendment to the U.S. Constitution in 1920. It would be the law of the land until its repeal in 1933.

Virginia went dry three years before national Prohibition began, with the state enacting laws prohibiting alcohol on Halloween night 1916.

Also check out chapter 4 for a list of Prohibition lingo.

repeal: The Twenty-First Amendment to the U.S. Constitution took effect on December 5, 1933, repealing Prohibition. When he signed it into law, President Franklin D. Roosevelt quipped, "What America needs now is a drink." The next year, in 1934, A. Smith Bowman Distillery began producing its first batch of Virginia Gentleman bourbon in rural Fairfax County; it's still produced to this date.

Ingredients (Non-Alcoholic)

bitters: A usually alcoholic solution comprising botanicals like bark, herbs, roots and the like, resulting in a concentrated liquid used in cocktails and other beverages with bitter flavors.

garnish: An item—such as a celery stalk, lemon or lime wedges, a sprig of mint or maraschino cherry—used to decorate or flavor a drink. Among the more common garnishes are citrus wedges, cut from fresh fruit such as lemon, lime or orange, perched on the rim of a glass, as with bloody marys and margaritas, and then squeezed and dropped in when served. Another common garnish is the citrus wheel, also known as a citrus slice, which is prepared and used much like a wedge with drinks such as a Long Island iced tea or a Tom Collins.

A twist is also an often-used garnish, where a very thin strip of citrus peel is draped on the side of a cocktail glass or added directly to the drink, not only adding color but also adding flavor due to the concentrated aromatic oils. Twists are seen in drinks such as cosmopolitans and martinis.

ice: Around the turn of the nineteenth century, the ice trade, also known as the frozen water trade, began offering ice to communities across the Eastern Seaboard and into the Caribbean that had not had access to it before or had limited access to it. As a result, many new eats and drinks were introduced, including iced drinks available either year-round or mostly year-round. Eventually, the trade spread, led by New England businessman Frederic Tudor. With the advent of electricity by the end of the nineteenth century, ice became more readily available.

Ice is recognized as an important element in many cocktails, whether to quickly cool down a drink while it is being crafted, as in a shaker, or to be placed in a glass with the cocktail mixture itself, melting and becoming part of the drink itself. Many bartenders carefully consider the makeup, shape and size of ice when constructing drinks.

mixer: A non-alcoholic beverage used in a mixed drink, such as juice (like orange juice and tomato juice), soda (like cola and ginger ale), sour mix and sparkling water (including club soda and tonic).

simple syrup: A liquid sweetening agent usually prepared by heating equal parts sugar (or other sweetener, such as honey or maple syrup) with water.

It can be flavored with other elements, such as cinnamon sticks, vanilla beans and the like. It is favored by bartenders in sweetening drinks because it blends well rather than having to dissolve as with granulated sugar. It will keep, covered and refrigerated, for up to a month.

sour mix: A mixture of sweet and sour elements used in many cocktails such as margaritas and vodka sours and whiskey sours. Traditionally it is equal parts lemon and/or lime juice with simple syrup (see above). The sour mix is added to a cocktail shaker with ice, and, optionally egg whites to create a foam, and shaken vigorously to incorporate. Also see "sour" in "Types of Drinks."

tonic: A carbonated water that is bitter due to the addition of quinine (from cinchona bark, used in medicine) and used as a mixer with such liquors as gin, as in a gin and tonic cocktail. Sometimes it is imbibed separately as a digestif (see "digestif" in "Types of Drinks").

PLACES

bar: Rising from the inns and taverns of the seventeenth and eighteenth centuries, the bar, also called a saloon and sometimes a pub, emerged as a place to spend leisure time, particularly enjoying alcoholic beverages. Unlike the inns and taverns before them, which had a focus on eats and lodging as well as drinks, bars, which sometimes offered food service, focused more on drinking. Some continued to be called taverns into the twentieth century, although they had little to do with the business model of their predecessor.

blind tiger: A place where illicit alcohol is sold, either by the bottle or by the drink. The space is not limited to being a sit-down establishment like nip joint or speakeasy, although the term was often interchangeable. It is also sometimes called a blind pig.

Sometimes a blind tiger could be a building, store or even an outdoor location used as pick up/drop off location. It gets its name from the premise of paying "admission" to see a natural curiosity, like a blind animal, such as a pig or a tiger, in which the proprietor throws in a drink for free. Remember, drinking alcohol during Prohibition was not technically illegal, only selling it, so the premise was used to circumvent the law. It often didn't work—not surprisingly, the establishments lacked a pig or tiger. Also see "nip joint" and "speakeasy."

distillery: The place where distilling of spirits is done. The first noted distillation of spirits in what would become English-speaking America took place in 1620 at Berkeley Plantation between Jamestown and Richmond by colonist George Thorpe. Today, there are more than seventy distilleries across Virginia, producing spirits from aqua vitae to bourbon, gin, liqueurs, moonshine, rye, sake and bourbon.

inn: This name began springing up in the late seventeenth century to indicate that lodging was available, providing a distinction from a tavern, which might offer some overnight accommodations but increasingly meant a place for eats and drinks only. Inns usually did offer food, too, not only to guests but also to the public at large.

nip joint: This usually referred to an illegal operation where a person could come to a place, often a residence, for a quick drink or two, typically with no amenities offered. Today, nip joints are often found in Appalachia, and the alcohol of choice is moonshine. A nip joint is a type of speakeasy. Sometimes the term "blind tiger" is used interchangeably. Also see "nip" in "Alcohol and Related" section.

ordinary: One of the early terms for taverns, generally interchangeable. By late in the seventeenth century and early eighteenth century, many began favoring the name tavern over ordinary. Also see "tavern."

speakeasy: A place where alcoholic beverages are sold illegally. Speakeasies rose greatly in popularity during Prohibition, and often there was great care before admission was granted—sometimes secret entrances and secret passwords were employed. Also see "blind tiger" and "nip joint."

tavern: A term that grew in favor in the late seventeenth century to describe a place to grab a bite to eat and a drink. Many taverns would accommodate overnight guests too, but increasingly the word *inn* was used to differentiate between a waypoint for eats and drinks and lodging. Also see "ordinary."

PROCESSES AND PROCEDURES

aging: The act of storing distilled spirits in barrels for a period of time to allow them to mellow and add flavor profiles from the cask's wood.

Bartenders also age batches of cocktails for shorter periods of time for much the same purpose. Also see "cask" in "Alcohol and Related."

distillation: The process of making spirits by separating substances from a liquid by boiling and through evaporation and condensation.

flame: To ignite a cocktail or shot, usually a thin layer of spirits is floated on top, for dramatic flair and sometimes to alter the flavor of the drink. Flaming cocktails have been noted for several centuries, and in the 1862 *How to Mix Drinks* cocktail book by Jerry Thomas, the author gave a recipe for the Blue Blazer, a Scotch-based hot toddy turned into a "blazing stream of liquid fire."

Fire is used in many Tiki culture drinks, especially when an alcohol-soaked sugar cube is placed in a citrus shell and floated in a signature boozy, tropical drink. Fire and sugar also play a big factor in the louching process with absinthe.

float: The layering of liquor or other ingredient on top of a cocktail or shot; also known as "pousse-café." This technique can provide a visual effect, as well as alter the flavor of the drink. Also see "layer."

free pour: A method by which bartenders pour alcohol into a glass or cocktail shaker by hand, counting the rate of flow rather than measuring the liquor by use of a jigger. Also see "jigger" in "Types of Drinks."

frost: The act of dipping a glass in water, draining it and placing it in the freezer to create a thin layer of frost around it, enhancing the beverage that will be served inside.

layer: Similar to float, this is the layering of various liqueurs in a glass to create a visual array of colors. Also see "float."

proof: The measure of alcohol in an alcoholic beverage. The strength of alcohol is represented by a number twice the percent by volume of the alcohol present; for example, a bottle of bourbon that is 80 proof is 40 percent ABV (alcohol by volume).

rim: Many cocktails call for the rimming of the edge of the glass, such as rimming the edge of a bloody mary with Old Bay seasoning, the edge of a margarita with salt or the edge of dessert cocktails with sugar.

To rim a glass, first moisten the glass edge. This can be done by running a wet paper towel around the rim or citrus wedge, or similar. Put what you are going to rim the glass with—salt, sugar and the like—on a small shallow plate and dip the glass down in it to coat.

shaken or stirred: It's an age-old debate: shaken or stirred? It seems there is more to it than personal preference, as some components in cocktails do better with one method over the other.

A cocktail is typically shaken when the drink includes bold, heavy or numerous ingredients—think eggs and dairy, fruit juices, liqueurs (also see "shaker" in "Alcohol and Related"), simple syrups (also see "shaker" in "Ingredients"), sour mixes and the like. The vigorous motion inside a shaker (also see "shaker" in "Equipment"), coupled with ice, work to quickly blend and cool the drink. This works for drinks like the cosmopolitan, mai tai and margarita.

Conversely, a cocktail is typically stirred when the drink is composed of spirits only or spirits and light mixers. The stirring is done for a shorter amount of time, as the viscosity of liquids are such that they do not require as much motion to combine. Some cocktails are even built in the glass over the ice. Examples of stirred cocktails, or cocktails built in the glass, include a Manhattan, martini and negroni.

TYPES OF DRINKS

aperitif: An alcoholic drink enjoyed before a meal, often as an appetizer. Examples include champagne or other sparkling wine or a liqueur (see "shaker" in "Alcohol and Related"). Also see "digestif."

call drink: An alcoholic drink in which one specifically asks for, or calls for, the exact name brand or brands of the liquors used in its crafting.

chaser: An alcoholic beverage of a different sort, either weaker or stronger, immediately served following the consumption of one alcoholic beverage, such as a boilermaker—this classic pairing consists of a shot of bourbon with a beer chaser.

cobbler: A popular nineteenth-century cocktail, noted as perhaps the first shaken drink, which launched the popularity of ice and straws into popular culture. Composed of a spirit (such as rum), sugar, crushed ice (noted as "cobbles") and fruit, it was noted by Charles Dickens as early as 1842. It remained popular through Prohibition.

digestif: An alcoholic drink enjoyed after a meal, often as dessert. Examples include a brandy or a liqueur (see "shaker" in "Alcohol and Related"). Also see "aperitif."

fizz: A variation on a sour cocktail, with the addition of carbonated water to give fizz. See "sour."

highball: A cocktail served in a tall glass and composed of liquor, such as whiskey, with water or carbonated beverage such as cola or ginger ale, over ice (see "highball" in "Equipment, including Glassware"). See "rickey."

neat: An alcoholic drink enjoyed without ice, as opposed to on the rocks. The drink is also referred to as served straight, straight up or up.

night cap: An alcoholic drink enjoyed at the end of the evening.

on the rocks: An alcoholic drink enjoyed with ice, as opposed to neat (also see "rocks glass" in "Equipment, including Glassware").

rickey: A favorite drink of the nineteenth century, with ties to Shoomaker's bar in Washington, D.C., and Democratic lobbyist Colonel Joe Rickey in the 1800s. This highball cocktail is made with gin or bourbon (the original was crafted with bourbon), half a lime squeezed and dropped in the glass and carbonated water. Seldom is sugar added to a rickey. See "highball."

shot, shooter: A shot of either hard liquor, a liqueur or a blend of liquor, liqueurs and/or mixers, served in a shot glass. There is also an oyster shooter, in which a raw oyster is placed in a shot glass and an alcoholic liquid, as well as often other ingredients such as bloody mary mix and/or hot sauce, is added. Contents in the shot glasses are consumed in one quick throw back (also see Shot Glass in "Equipment, including Glassware").

sling: A drink strongly associated with Tiki culture, the sling has ties to Singapore at the turn of the twentieth century. It is traditionally a gin-based cocktail sweetened with sugar, accented with lemon or lime juice and capped with sparkling water or ginger ale.

smash: A type of julep, the premise of this nineteenth-century cocktail is to take fresh ingredients such as fruit and herbs, smash them and serve them in a glass with sugar or simple syrup (see "simple syrup" in "Ingredients") and a spirit of choice, often bourbon or rye, then packed with crushed or shaved ice. In his 1862 *How to Mix Drinks*, Jerry Thomas gave a recipe for a whiskey smash that included lemon, spearmint, simple syrup, bourbon and plenty of ice. "This beverage is simply a julep on a small plan," he noted.

sour: There is a variety of drinks that fall under the sour category, drinks that, in part, are made with a sour mix. These are drinks that have a sweetness and a tartness to them, the most common being the daiquiri, margarita, sidecar and whiskey sour. Sours have been around for some time, described in Jerry Thomas's 1862 cocktail authority *How to Mix Drinks* (also see "sour mix" in "Ingredients").

toddy: A favorite beverage since at least the eighteenth century, and one with strong ties to Colonial Virginia, the toddy, also known as the hot toddy, was originally called the "taddy." A recipe in 1786 defined it as a "beverage made of alcoholic liquor with hot water, sugar, and spices." Over time, it's become a chicken noodle soup of sorts, with a purported cure-all property, especially for colds and related ailments. One thing is certain: it warms from the insides out, one thing our forefathers definitely knew.

well drink: Also known as a rail drink, this is an alcoholic drink in which one does not specifically ask for a particular name brand or brands of the liquors used in its crafting and leaves the choice up to the bartender, who uses one of the lower-cost "house brands." The space in which a bartender works is typically called either the rail or well, and a number of spirits are stocked for general use when one is not specified (also see "call drink").

LIST OF RECIPES

In order presented.

Chapter 1: The Seventeenth Century

Bumbo
Flip
Grog
Made-Good Punch
Milk Punch
Rattle-Skull
Strawberry Shrub
Stone Fence
Rum Balls

Chapter 2. The Eighteenth Century

Excellent Cherry Bounce
Bourbon Slush
George Washington's Egg Nog (with Rum-Infused Whipped Cream)
Fish House Punch
Haute Chocolate

Rye and Ginger
Sangaree and Sangaree Ice
Mulled Wine
Wassail
Hot Buttered Rum

Chapter 3. The Nineteenth Century

Apple Cobbler
Gin Fix
The Virginia Fizz
The Grover
Essentials for a Mint Julep
A Most Marvelous Mint Julep
An Old Fashioned Sling
Whiskey Smash
Gin Rickey
Whiskey Sour
Teetotaler Lemonade
Tom & Jerry

Chapter 4. The Twentieth Century

Apple Pie Shine
Viva La Cuba Libre
Pretty in Pink Lady
Blue Hawaii
A Mid-Century Modern–ish Martini
Long Island Iced Tea
Sex on Virginia Beach
Candy Apple-tini

Chapter 5. The Twenty-First Century

We Got the Beet-tini
Storm's Brewin' (with Category Five Moonshine Cherries)

LIST OF RECIPES

G + K (Gin + Kombucha)
Boys to the Yard Boozy Milkshake (with Bourbon Whipped Cream)
Caribbean Queen Spritz
Quarantini

y213

BIBLIOGRAPHY

Other publications and archived and contemporaneous newspaper and magazine articles, as well as internet-based information, were also relied on for research for this book.

Austin, Gregory A. *Alcohol in Western Society from Antiquity to 1800: A Chronological History*. Santa Barbara, CA: ABC-Clio Information Services, 1985.

Brown, John Hull. *Early American Beverages: The Origin of Drink and Cocktail*. New York: Bonanza Books, 1966.

Covert, Adrian. *Taverns of the American Revolution: The Battles, the Booze and the Barrooms of the Revolutionary War*. San Rafael, CA: Insight Editions, 2016.

Dabney, Joseph Earl. *Mountain Spirits: A Chronicle of Corn Whiskey and the Southern Appalachian Moonshine Tradition*. Charleston, SC: The History Press, 2014.

Evans-Hylton, Patrick. *Classic Restaurants of Coastal Virginia*. Charleston, SC: The History Press, 2019.

———. *Dishing Up Virginia: 145 Recipes that Celebrate Colonial Traditions and Contemporary Flavors*. North Adams, MA: Storey Publishing, 2013.

Foster, Mary L. *Colonial Capitals of the Dominion of Virginia*. Lynchburg, VA: J.P. Bell Company, 1906.

Furnas, J.C. *The Life and Times of the Late Demon Rum: Tracing the Change in American Attitudes Toward Alcohol*. New York: Capricorn Books, 1965.

Grasse, Steven. *Colonial Spirits: A Revolutionary Drinking Guide*. New York: Abrams, 2016.

Grimes, William. *Straight Up or On the Rocks: The Story of the American Cocktail*. New York: North Point Press, 2001.

Harwell, Richard Barksdale. *The Mint Julep: The Origin of the Mint Julep*. Charlottesville: University Press of Virginia, 1975.

Lathrop, Elise. *Early American Inns and Taverns: Take a Look at Inns, Hostels and Taverns*. New York: Arno Press, 1977.

Murdock, Catherine Gilbert. *Domesticating Drink: Women, Men and Alcohol in America, 1870–1940*. Baltimore, MD: Johns Hopkins University Press, 1998.

Okrent, Daniel. *Last Call: Rise and Fall of Prohibition*. New York: Scribner, 2010.

Parramore, Thomas G., with Peter C. Stewart and Tommy L. Bogger. *Norfolk: The First Four Centuries*. Charlottesville: University of Virginia Press, 2000.

Pearson, C.C., and J. Edwin Hendricks. *Liquor and Anti-Liquor in Virginia, 1619–1919: The Hostility of Liquor Among Middle Class People*. Durham, NC: Duke University Press, 1967.

Pogue, Dennis J. *Founding Spirits: George Washington and the Beginnings of the American Whiskey Industry*. Buena Vista, VA: Harbor Books, 2011.

Randolph, Mary. *The Virginia House-Wife. With Historical Notes and Commentaries by Karen Hess*. Columbia: University of South Carolina Press, 1984.

Rorabaugh, W.J. *The Alcoholic Republic: An American Tradition*. New York: Oxford University Press, 1979.

Shearer, Kathy. *Tales from the Moonshine Trade: Southwest Virginia Moonshine Whiskey*. Emory, VA: Clinch Mountain Press, 2011.

Tazewell, William L. *Norfolk's Waters: An Illustrated Maritime History of Hampton Roads*. Woodland Hills, CA: Windsor Publications, 1982.

Thompson, Peter. *Rum Punch and Revolution: Taverngoing and Public Life in Eighteenth-Century Philadelphia*. Philadelphia: University of Pennsylvania Press, 1999.

Tucker, George Holbert. *More Tidewater Landfalls*. Norfolk, VA: Donning Company Publishers, 1975.

———. *Norfolk Highlights*. Norfolk, VA: Norfolk Historical Society, 1972.

INDEX

ABOUT THE AUTHOR

Patrick Evans-Hylton is a Johnson & Wales–trained chef, food historian, Certified Bourbon Steward and award-winning food writer, covering tasty trends since 1995 in print, broadcast and electronic media. He is the publisher of virginiaeatsanddrinks.com.

In 2019, Evans-Hylton's website launched Four Farthing Spiced Rum in partnership with Chesapeake Bay Distillery. This historically inspired rum harkens back to the days when tall ships lined the Norfolk waterfront, then known as Four Farthing Point, with exotic spices from the Caribbean, including ingredients to make America's first drink: rum. Find out more at Evans-Hylton's website.

Evans-Hylton eats, drinks and writes in his Chesapeake Bay kitchen in Virginia Beach with his four-legged sous chef, Miss Pico de Gallo, a Chihuahua.

For additional content—such as bartender and distiller interviews, cocktail recipes and more, plus updates on this book—visit virginiadistilled.com or virginiaeatsanddrinks.com.

Visit us at
www.historypress.com